Stay Married for Life

9 Joy-filled Steps to a Great Relationship

DAN SEABORN & PETER NEWHOUSE
WITH SUSAN LEWIS AND LISA VELTHOUSE

Stay Married for Life

Published by AACC Press
Forest, VA

ISBN-13: 978-0-9816788-1-8

Printed in the United States of America

Contents

Acknowledgments

Dan says:

Most of what I know about marriage comes from the walks that my wife Jane and I share together. We've had some of our best talks and worst arguments walking. There have been times when we've held hands and displayed a love to marvel about. Other times she's been twenty yards ahead of me and we're both steaming. And through it all, we've grown deeper and deeper with each other and in Christ. Jane, one of my favorite things in life is to see you strapping on those walking shoes—thanks, babe.

To my children—Alan, Josh, Crissy, and Anna Elizabeth—who have been far more understanding than I deserve: I am thankful for your commitment to loving me and helping me grow. I love you!

Dr. Peter says:

I give thanks and am grateful for what I have been given as a husband, father, and counselor. I am truly a blessed man to have Shawn Maree for a life mate—she is an amazing person and wife, and she makes me a better person. I am also incredibly humbled by having three children: Megan Maree, Isaak Peter, and Sophia Christine. They are awesome, they encourage me, and they give me a great reason to have a growing marriage. Lastly, I am thankful to work in a place where I feel affirmed, valued, and encouraged to stay true to my faith.

Foreword

Stay married for life! I couldn't think of a more fitting title to describe the heart of every love-struck newlywed. Think about it: how many people get married with the thought in mind that the relationship may only last a few years? That's silly. Yet, for many reasons, only half make it the distance. And if you try to tally up those who actually "live joyfully with the one they love all the days of their life," the numbers get ugly.

Studies completed over the years have all pointed to a decline in income, values, and morality where divorce is present. A University of Chicago study reports that in cities with populations over 100,000, the crime level is lowered when the rate of divorce is lower. Another study by the University of Michigan revealed that family income drops an average of 28 to 42% when there is a divorce. It has also been studied and reported that boys living without fathers in the home are two to three times more likely to commit crimes that result in jail time.[1]

That's why we all need to care about marriage in America and to participate where we can to help people stay married for life. We can sit back and let the situation continue to slide downhill, or we can proactively develop a strategy to do something about it. If we are going to win the war for marriage, we have a lot of work to do. As Stonewall Jackson said, "We have to get everything in the fight." *Stay Married for Life* takes a bold step in that direction.

---

1   The Heritage Foundation. *New study details harmful effects of divorce on American society.* Retrieved from http://www.heritage.org/research/reports/2000/06/new-study-details-harmful-effects-of-divorce-on-american-society on August 10, 2011.

National speaker, pastor, author, and founder of Winning At Home, Dan Seaborn collaborates with psychologist and director of the Winning At Home Family Wellness Center, Dr. Peter Newhouse, to explore in nine joyful steps how couples can stay married for life. The honesty, humor, and hands-on approach in their writing will provide simple solutions to what might be considered complex problems in marriage. Their knowledge stems from the experience of working and counseling with couples for more than 25 years.

Saving marriage in America is an overwhelming thought. That's why I encourage you to take the first step and work on your own marriage so it can speak to others. The first chapter will help you understand the need to cherish your spouse more than other things in your life. It will help you to see and understand how your marriage morphs from giddy newlyweds to the OK-the-honeymoon-is-over stage and how to joyfully live within that reality. The beauty of their approach is that the authors don't pile on more to-do's to accomplish that, but show you how to do it with less.

Money continues to be one of the top three reasons people get divorced and in Chapter two, the authors explore how each gender views finances and why these opposing views cause so many disharmonies in a relationship.

 Chapter 3 follows up with another hot and fiery topic—sexual satisfaction. The root of most sexual problems between a husband and wife originate from their differing "sexpectations", as the authors refer to them. They believe that once couples better understand each other and their different ideas about romance and sensuality, sex can be the wonderful gift God intended it to be for married couples.

In the rest of the chapters, Seaborn and Newhouse discuss the importance of spending time together, developing genuine friendship by hitting the bull's-eye on the friendship target, valuing physical attractiveness, finding emotional connectedness, and guarding home harmony.

The final and most important chapter relates to building spiritual fusion. Seaborn and Newhouse reveal the secret of how fusion helps couples to accomplish, understand, and implement all the ideas brought forth in the other chapters.

Once you get your marriage to a successful point, talk about it positively to your friends, family, neighbors and co-workers. Share with them that through time, effort, and a commitment to make it work, marriage can be a beautiful relationship between a man and a woman. This will give them hope and encouragement that marriage is a worthy and beneficial venture and will be another step in helping couples stay married for life.

Tim Clinton

Introduction

The Importance of Staying Married for Life

The decline of marriage over the last 20 years cannot be attributed to just one single source. There are a variety of contributing factors that have led to the demise of an institution that is the foundation of a society. A few years ago, *Time* magazine and the Pew Research Center released a poll showing that nearly four in ten Americans think "marriage is obsolete."

As a nation, we are unfazed by climbing divorce rates and oblivious to the decline in family values. We seemed to have forgotten God's beautiful design for marriage between a committed man and woman. We hope that will change for you after reading this book.

The adoption of no-fault divorce, higher-than-ever marital expectations and cohabitation are some of the catalysts that have triggered a high divorce rate. Cohabitation alone has risen more than 74% since 2000. And while cohabitates believe they are setting themselves up for success by "trying out" the marriage scenario before tying the knot, there is a higher divorce rate among couples who live together before marriage than couples who don't. With each marriage that fails in America, the bedrock of our society slowly erodes.

This book, however, is not a statistical analysis of why marriage is failing, but rather a simple, nine-step approach that we hope will help save marriage in America. What does it take to stay happily married for life? It's a question, we the authors, had to ask ourselves for our own marriages. Professionally, in our roles as a speaker (Dan) and a counselor (Peter), nearly every day we meet couples who are struggling to make their marriages work. The search for a good, lasting relationship is universal and as regular guys and husbands ourselves, we know how important this search is because we strive to stay married to our own wives—happily and for life!

In writing this book, we each brought our own personal experience in marriage—trial and error, successes and failures and combined it with what we'd both observed in our professional interactions with couples. Then we spent some time examining key features of lasting marriages and in the end what we had compiled was a finely-tuned list of nine. This book is that list: nine practices that can bring joy and longevity to a couple's relationship.

It's not only important to us that your marriage succeed, but it's critical to the stability of our country that all marriages thrive and prosper. Marriage builds community while divorce tears them down and that should matter to all of us.

Therefore, the goal of this book is to promote marriage and to provide couples with nine joy-filled steps that we believe are necessary to help keep you married for life and to save marriage in America.

THE CONCEPT

People can acquire many things during life, but nearly every person has a certain object or group of objects he or she values most. Heirlooms, collectibles, photos, memorabilia, trinkets once touched by famous people—anything with sentiment attached to it can become a treasure. These are the things we keep in protected spaces and protected cases, far away from any possibility of damage or fingerprints.

We protect these things because we cherish them.

We cherish them because they're valuable. They're worth something to us.

This raises the question: What's marriage worth to you?

THE CONSTİTUENTS

In an informal survey of couples, we asked, "In your marriage, who has more desire to be cherished/valued?" Responses:

The Husband: 5%
The Wife: 39%
Both: 55%

Chapter 1

Establishing
Cherishing Attitudes

The American way has taught us that you must earn a living, earn a degree, and even earn respect, but is cherishing your spouse something you need to earn?

Americans take great pride in earning what they consider their material goods. Perhaps it stems from the period of The Great Depression which dragged Americans down by taking everything they owned, including their dignity. However, the Industrial Revolution was instrumental in picking them up again and many Americans garnered great wealth. It's possible this new found affluence was the beginning of a change from a "we" to a "me" society, as people who had lived through the depression were determined to hold on even tighter to the things they owned.

They began cherishing their stuff more than the people in the lives. This attitude continues today and is the reason marriage can be so difficult.

Remember how in the beginning, you both were ecstatic to experience anything the other person enjoyed. Every day you wanted to learn more about him or her, and practically everything you learned made your new love seem more endearing. You cherished every moment together.

When he told you he loved Elvis, you memorized all the lyrics to "Heartbreak Hotel." When you found out she liked steak more than seafood, you made reservations at the best grill joint in town. When he complimented a certain perfume or cologne, you bought the jug and drenched yourself in it. You even got excited about going to her youngest cousin's piano recital.

In the early days, if your spouse did something annoying or irritating, you chalked it up to a vibrant personality and overlooked the incident. If he behaved like a bratty little kid, you gave him the benefit of the doubt—he probably had a bad day at work. If she disagreed with you on an issue, you were quick to get past it. You probably even credited her brilliance in the process. Everything was fine. After all, your spouse was so cute back then.

It's amazing how perspectives can change, isn't it?

At the Beginning

Neither one anticipated that it would be like this. When Tim and Heather[2] had their fairy-tale wedding a few months ago, they expected married life to be just a better version of what they had when they were dating and engaged. After "I do," the couple walked down the church aisle arm in arm, beaming from ear to ear under a shower of flower petals.

Seven months later, Heather told Tim she'd been keeping a secret from him. Before their wedding, she'd been embarrassed to disclose the exact total on her credit card statements. She had worried about making Tim share the burden of her own debt. Still, she said, she was ready to come clean, to the tune of about three thousand dollars. Heather figured Tim would be upset at her confession, but she never

---

2 Certain details in this book, including names, have been changed in order to conceal the identities of the subjects.

would have guessed that he'd ask her to move out of the house. Yet that is exactly what he did, and that's why Heather, a bride of less than a year, has been living at her sister's house lately.

Like most couples, Tim and Heather had high hopes at the start of their marriage. Like most couples, they wanted it to work out. They expected it would be great. They intended to happily remain together forever, to be loving each other for life. They thought their first year together would be bliss.

Before all this happened, Tim didn't believe his wife would ever withhold the truth from him, as Heather didn't believe her husband would ever ask her to leave their home. But she did. And then he did.

As for all couples, at the beginning of Tim and Heather's journey, the scenery was beautiful in every direction and the road to bliss stretched toward the horizon like something straight out of *Sleeping Beauty*. When these two embarked on their journey, everything seemed thrilling and new, happy and hopeful. The gear on their backs was shiny and crisp and dirt free from lack of use. But they had only strapped on their marital hiking boots. They had yet to realize that trail blisters and sore muscles were right around the next bend.

No More CHDs

Marriage has the uncanny ability to replace romance with reality, and *fast*. For most couples, it's the shock of a lifetime. At any given matrimonial moment, one spouse is upset and the other doesn't have a clue why. One wants conversation; the other wants quiet. One wants to go out; the other wants to stay in. One wants to have sex; the other wants to remodel the basement. It's one gigantic argument waiting to happen.

If you've been married more than a month, it's fair to guess that you've already passed the point of CHDs (constant happy discoveries). You've begun a new era in which you notice things about your spouse that are a bit less than lovely. In fact, some of the things your spouse does can be absolutely infuriating.

Maybe he left the toilet seat up on four different occasions yesterday. Maybe last week her lipstick went through the dryer and ruined all your pants. Maybe he snores so loudly that at times two pillows over each ear won't begin to muffle the sound. Maybe when she's mad, she shoots you glares from across the table that could kill. Maybe he spends half his Saturdays watching football and yelling at the TV. Maybe sometimes things dangle from her nose.

In light of what you know today, the head-over-heels era of your relationship might seem ridiculous or even foolish by comparison. After all, the things you found endearing in those days are the same things that drive you berserk now. Still, while your opinion of marriage might be much more realistic these days compared to what it used to be, that doesn't necessarily mean something has gone wrong.

In the Land of Limbo

When people venture beyond the single world, before they really enter married territory, they often experience a nice little in-between. It's a land of limbo, and its inhabitants are so unique they have their own label: *newlyweds*. The differences between newlyweds and married people are easily distinguishable:

Newlyweds leave love notes on the kitchen table if they have to go away for twenty minutes.
Married people might leave the house for six hours without thinking to tell their spouse where they're going or when they'll be back.

Newlyweds still lock the door and use air freshener in the bathroom.
Married people have seen it all and have smelled it all. Why waste time closing or freshening?

Newlyweds will spend three days planning and cooking their spouse's favorite six-course meal.
Married people buy microwavable dinners.

Newlyweds will spend all their cash on cards and candy for their spouse.
Married people buy lawn equipment.

When newlyweds have their first fight, they spend days making up.
When married people have a fight, they can get over it and start another one in less than five minutes.

It can be scary to realize you've moved beyond the newlywed phase because joining the ranks of married people isn't nearly so glamorous. Married people encounter things about marriage that don't seem the least bit fun, exciting, or sexy. They experience times when the person they married doesn't always look nice, smell nice, or act nice. They've realized that the honeymoon really does end, that at some point the wrapping paper from the wedding gifts needs to be picked up off the floor. They've discovered that there are moments when "I love you so much, sweetheart" gets traded in for "Where did you put the remote?"

It's hard work being a married person. Navigating through the highs and lows of marital terrain is no small feat. The journey is long. Some days feel as if your compass is busted. And at times, marriage feels as if you're not only trying to survive together; you're also trying to survive each other.

Surviving Each Other

It doesn't make a difference if you dated for fifteen years or if you went to premarital therapy with the best counselors in the history of the world or if you scored 100 percent on the latest *Cosmo* compatibility test; you're still going to have problems relating to and understanding your spouse. Why? Because you're people. Because you're people who happen to have flaws, but mostly because you're people. And no two people will ever be able to completely agree on everything.

Jay and Vivian had been married less than a year when the argument happened. Actually, it was less of an argument than it was a confrontation. Regardless, decades later the night is still legendary for both of them. They laugh about it on a regular basis, they tell their kids about it, and they do their best *not* to relive it.

If you ask about that night, Vivian will tell you that Jay was angry with her about something—she can't remember what—and he seemed to expect that she should know why he was upset. (Jay doesn't remember the specifics either, but he does admit he was pouting about something.) For the life of her, Vivian couldn't figure out what she'd done wrong, so she asked her husband to shed some light on the issue. In response, he gave her the silent treatment.

Invalidations . . . span a broad range, including what we do, what we say, what we don't do, and what we don't say.

"I was holding it in," says Jay with a chuckle, "like we men tend to do— except she didn't want me to hold it in."

Annoyed by the silence coming from the other side of the bed, Vivian repeatedly asked to know what had gone wrong. Jay repeatedly responded by ignoring her. So Vivian worked up all the strength she could muster in one arm, wound up, and hit her husband's shoulder as hard as she could. "I just hauled off and blasted him," she says. "I've never hit anybody like that in my whole life!" With a look toward Jay and a mischievous giggle, she continues. "It probably didn't hurt his arm at all, but it sure hurt my hand."

"Let's just put it this way," her husband says. "It's not like I was fearful of getting hit again."

Hearing them tell the story, it's clear Vivian and Jay can look back on the old days and have a good laugh. Why shouldn't they? Their marriage is worlds different now. They've both worked hard at improving their conflict resolution skills—no more silent treatment, no more hitting. It's worked wonders, to the point that both of them get a kick out of the argument story these days.

On the night it happened, though, there wasn't much amusement. After the hit heard 'round the world, Jay kept his back to his wife and kept his mouth shut until he dozed off. And Vivian rolled over, stinging hand and all, and went to sleep.

Invalidations

Not unlike many other couples in the world, Jay and Vivian "solved" their disagreement by ending it with a tactic we call invalidating. Rather than coming together and working toward common ground, they drew a line in the sand and set up camp on opposing sides. Then they started hurling invalidations[3] at each other.

Invalidations, as the word suggests, are behaviors that take value away from people. They span a broad range, including what we do, what we say, what we don't do, and what we don't say. They can be big things or slight things—some of them are glaringly obvious; others are visible only to a well-trained eye.

The following are several examples of common invalidations:

Blatant Slams

- Rolling your eyes, glaring, name-calling, using curse words or sarcasm toward your spouse
- Creating uncomplimentary nicknames, criticizing your spouse's weight/ appearance/skills, mocking his or her intelligence, complaining

---

3 This term has been used before, by Drs. H. Markman and S. Stanley of the Center for Marital and Family Studies and the Prevention and Relationship Enhancement Program (PREP). See www.du.edu/psychology/marriage/index.htm.

Slamming by Association

- Ridiculing your spouse's friends, family members, occupation, or gender
- Belittling your spouse's beliefs, projects, or creations

Comparisons

- Insulting by saying, "You're just like your mother [father, brother, sister, friend]."
- Suggesting that as a couple your social status doesn't measure up to others'
- Commenting positively to your wife about another woman's appearance
- Commenting positively to your husband about another man's appearance

Physical Aggression[4]

- Slamming a fist, kicking a wall or another object, peeling out of a parking lot, slamming a door
- Standing over your spouse, throwing an object, cruelly immobilizing your spouse
- Slapping, hitting, punching, shoving, or kicking your spouse

Negative Interpretations, Labels, and Expectations

- Assuming the worst or expecting the worst from your spouse in a given situation
- Using "You always . . ." or "You never . . . " as ammunition in an argument

---

4 Under no circumstances do we believe a person should abuse or intentionally harm another person. Such actions are intolerable. Many forms of physical aggression are excessive to the point that they are never warranted—they cross the line into dangerously hurtful (not to mention illegal) behavior. If a person is being abused, he or she should seek safety, professional counsel, and the aid of law enforcement.

- Neglecting to notice how well your spouse is doing
- Rehashing old arguments or mistakes

Withholding Self

- Refusing to listen or hear a spouse's comments
- Not reciprocating when a spouse offers affection
- Rejecting sexual advances of your spouse
- Failing to verbally express pleasure in your spouse: his or her talents, traits, or positive developments and changes
- Isolating yourself from your spouse physically or disconnecting emotionally

Take time individually to examine this list of invalidations. Give it a really good look. Now think back over the past month or so. In what way(s) have you invalidated your spouse? How often? Under what circumstances? In which locations? If you had to ask your husband or wife to answer the question for you, what would he or she say?

Now that you have your own personalized list of invalidations in mind, if you're anything like us, you're probably tempted to defend yourself and your actions:

I got caught up in the moment.

It's what we're both used to.

He/she hurt me first; I'm only retaliating.

It's the only way I can make him/her listen to me.

I didn't realize I was doing anything wrong.

I was upset.

I was angry.

It's no big deal anyway.

There's a whole array of excuses people can give in attempt to explain away invalidating behaviors. With all due respect, we don't want to talk about any of those reasons. Trust us, every single one is secondary at best because there's a much bigger reason going on here.

All invalidations have one thing in common. Each ridicule and each refusal, each unkind comparison and aggressive action, each rolled eye and negative assumption—they all begin in the same place.

The Root of All Invalidations

I (Peter) counsel with people full time at Winning At Home. Conflicting spouses are a regular part of my average day. Still, when Brad and Jill came to our offices for marital counseling, the initial session was especially rough. Upon entering my office, the very first thing they did was remove the throw pillows from the couch so, when they took their seats, they'd be as far away from each other as was physically possible. Then, when they did sit down, they clung to the furniture arm at their side, maximizing the distance between the two of them.

All through the session they glared at each other and made snide remarks. They were argumentative and negative, always assuming the worst from each other. After Brad told his side of the story, Jill snorted indignantly. Then Jill told her side while Brad shook his head, arms crossed over his chest the whole time.

By looking at these two, I could clearly see their main marital problem. There it was—the root of all the invalidations they were putting on display, from one suffocated armrest to the other. It was as obvious with Brad and Jill as it had been with countless couples before them, as obvious as it's been with countless couples after them: Neither spouse was cherishing the other.

A Downhill Battle

Take a moment and consider this: Of all your material possessions, which one is the most valuable to you? Is it a photo? A gift? A letter? A piece of clothing? A souvenir? Something you've had for a long time? Something you waited a long time to get?

I (Dan) own a basketball signed by NBA legends Michael Jordan, Shaquille O'Neal, Earvin "Magic" Johnson, and Larry Bird. I'm a basketball fanatic, so it's safe to say the ball is one of my favorite possessions. It is encased in Plexiglas, so grimy little fingers can't defile it, and stored high on a shelf. I wouldn't think about taking that ball outside for a shootaround—not in a million years. It's too valuable, too much of a treasure. I cherish it.

If you're like most other couples in the Western world, one of the biggest reasons you married your spouse is that you developed a cherishing attitude toward him or her. (Remember those CHDs we mentioned earlier?) Your thoughts about your spouse were strongly positive. You viewed him as a treasure, a prize. You took pleasure in her because she held importance, significance, and meaning in your life. Cherishing was likely a key part of your premarriage relationship. And if you want your marriage to be a lasting, loving one, cherishing should also play a key role in your lives after the wedding.

Your spouse wants to know that you find him or her to be worthy of a Plexiglas case and a prominent, protective spot on the highest shelf. A wife needs her husband to express her value to her. She needs to know that he sees worth in her—that she is precious, special, and important in his eyes. She wants to feel she is his prized possession, that he wouldn't give her up for anything. Similarly, a husband needs his wife to communicate his value to him. He needs to know that she sees worth in him—that he is capable, special, and important in her eyes. He wants to feel he is her prized possession, that she loves having him around.

All people have an innate desire to feel cherished, and failing to cherish your spouse cheats him or her out of having that desire fulfilled within your marriage. This is a very big deal. It's precisely why invalidations are so dangerous—because they cancel out anything that seems like cherishing. Hurtful conduct between spouses easily trumps kindness. Wounding words make a person forget the gentle ones. A single slap refutes hundreds of caresses.

But there's more. Not only do invalidations ruin the cherishing process on the receiving end, but they ruin it on the giving end as well. If you treat your spouse as if they are of little value, over time their recognized value will decrease even more.

It's like playing four quarters of street basketball with the legends' autographs. If I take Michael, Magic, Shaq, and Larry out from under glass and let them take a beating from the pavement grime, the backboard, and dirty hands, then that ball's price tag just dropped significantly, didn't it? Why? Because when I fail to treat something like a valuable item, it gets knocked around, and its value diminishes.

As if that weren't enough, there's one more thing. What couples often fail to realize is that almost any problem can instantly be made much worse when a few invalidations are stirred in. No matter what other troubles threaten a marriage—communication issues, financial woes, emotional baggage, problems in the bedroom, different personalities, or meddling in-laws—everything goes downhill.

When invalidations are thrown into the picture, they signal a couple is moving away from each other rather than toward each other. Instead of facing trials together as a team, the two people face each other, fighting as opponents. No longer are they focused on building their relationship together; instead, they've become distracted by their differences and disputes, caught up in defensiveness and retaliations. When one spouse fires, the other fires back: *If you hurt me, I'll hurt you.*

In no time at all, the husband and wife are caught up in a cycle of revenge, trading invalidations. In time, their revenge begins to devour them. Nearly every marital spat becomes entangled in the two spouses' efforts to demean each other. Still, rarely does either spouse try to stop the cycle. After all, how could they? They're both too busy keeping score.

Which Comes First?

One question lies at the heart of marital invalidation swaps: Why should one spouse cherish if the other won't? Or where does cherishing begin? Should we cherish in order to be cherished in return, or should we cherish as a response when we've been cherished already? Which comes first, the chicken or the cherishing?

Cherishing isn't a trade-off: "If I cherish him, then he'll cherish me" or "If I cherish her, then she'll cherish me." Cherishing is totally one-sided and fully selfless. It expects nothing in return. Nothing.

Cherishing is a frame of reference, a lens we use to color the things and people in our lives. It isn't a behavior as much as it's a perception, a way of seeing, a mind-set, an attitude. Having a cherishing attitude means that I value my spouse, regardless of the way I feel and regardless of the mood he or she is currently in. A cherishing attitude gives value regardless of what happened yesterday, last month, last year, or fifteen years ago. It means I treat my spouse as a person of value regardless of his or her mannerisms, traits, quirks, annoying habits, hang-ups, idiosyncrasies, inconsistencies, failures, extra pounds, garlic breath, onion breath, or bed head.

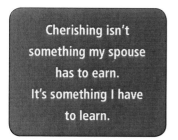

Cherishing isn't something my spouse has to earn. It's something I have to learn.

So, you see, cherishing doesn't depend on personality traits, and it isn't the result of a good mood. It isn't something you do only when you feel like it. It doesn't happen only when there's money in the bank, only when you feel successful, only when you're happy, or only when you feel cherished yourself. It isn't something you do only when you're in a good mood or only to get sex or only after sex. If you think those things are cherishing, you're missing the whole point. Cherishing isn't something my spouse has to *earn*. It's something I have to *learn*.

Does this mean cherishing turns me into a doormat? Does it imply that I should settle for mediocre in my marriage? That I should let broken promises slide? That I should allow another person to beat me up emotionally or physically? That I should tolerate life as it is—forever?

No, no, no, no, and not necessarily. It simply means that cherishing is a choice, and the choice is yours.

Regardless of who's at fault or who's to blame, you always have the option to cherish. In every marital situation you face, you can choose to see your spouse through a cherishing lens. You can choose to focus on the good qualities, to remember the better days, to aim for the best. If you learn to make this choice, it will transform your marriage. And it'll probably be much easier than you would've ever thought possible.

Trash Racks

If you've ever been to Hoover Dam, you know it's a fascinating thing to see. Its construction alone was unprecedented—workers used more than 5 million barrels of cement, 45 million pounds of reinforcement steel, and 840 miles of pipe and fitting to build it. The project was completed in 1935, but the dam was built so solidly that it's expected to last thousands of years.

Still, despite its strength and durability, Hoover Dam isn't indestructible. One particular concern of its designers had to do with erosion. With enormous volumes of water moving through pipes and hitting turbines for years and years on end, even cement and steel would surely wear down. Also, river water carries loads of debris. How would the structure tolerate that?

The solution: trash racks. Trash racks are huge metal grates that clear away debris, cutting down on erosion and blockage within the dam. Imagine trying to convert water into electricity amid loads of river debris—rocks and boulders, leaves, dead fish, rotting logs, fast-food cartons, and other trash. Think of how many potential repairs are eliminated by catching the rubble before it has a chance to enter the pipes. Consider all the excess time and energy needed to fix a damaged system. Think of how much erosion is spared—all due to a really big colander. Think of how much better the whole system is merely because of a few trash racks.

Well, there you have it. There's the answer for cherishing in your marriage.

The Goo Factor

Often when people decide to cherish their spouse, they begin by considering the goo factor: *How tender am I toward my spouse?* They think of little expressions of kindness: holding hands, whispering sweet nothings, stowing gifts under pillows, or composing sonnets. After a brief analysis of their current behavior, these people usually conclude that their goo factor isn't high enough to be classified as cherishing. So they vow to do more—more holding, more whispering, more stowing, or more composing. It's beyond sappy. Theirs is a valiant goal, but in the process of developing a whole new set of behaviors, these people totally miss the boat on cherishing.

> Ninety-five percent of cherishing is getting rid of the stuff that isn't cherishing.

Today most Americans barely have time to brush their teeth, let alone work on their marriage. For many, the thought of cherishing their spouse sounds like something to add to the already seemingly long list of things to do. The truth is, cherishing is an exercise in removing actions and building up positive results. In fact, you might even spend less time working on your marriage if you start cherishing your spouse. That's because 95 percent of cherishing is getting rid of the stuff that isn't cherishing.

The equation is simple. Instead of being more nice, more appropriate, more appreciative, and more pleasant, learn to be less unkind, less inappropriate, less unappreciative, and less unpleasant. The result could garner you an A+ marriage. Basically, if you want to get better at cherishing your spouse, the best thing you can do is to stop invalidating.

That's right—stop invalidating. Bite your bottom lip, blow off steam, walk away, let it go, resist the urge. Stop using that less-than-complimentary nickname. Stop rolling your eyes and sighing. Stop speaking poorly about your spouse and to your spouse. Hold your tongue when that nickname or those hurtful words are on their way out. Deny yourself permission to assume the worst. Forbid yourself from lashing out.

On the flip side, be forgiving when your spouse has a bad day. Quit with the sarcasm, the criticism, and the insults. Quit making fun. Quit talking about how good she *used* to look. Quit saying "always" and "never" in the midst of a brawl. Stop bringing up that old argument— let it die already. Stop withdrawing, stop withholding. Force yourself, despite every urge that screams otherwise, to stop invalidating. It will revolutionize—*revolutionize*—your marriage.

Chapter 1 Follow-up
Establishing Cherishing Attitudes

His & Hers:

- List your most prized possessions:

- In what ways do you cherish these objects more than your spouse?

Answer individually, then discuss together:

- As time passes in your marriage, are you getting better or worse at cherishing your spouse? In what ways?

- Cherishing is a learned behavior. What did you learn about cherishing from this chapter?

- This chapter points out that invalidations make other marital arguments bigger. How have you observed this in your relationship?

- When I invalidate my spouse, I usually do so by . . .

- The type of invalidation that is most hurtful to me is _____ because . . .

- I think the type of invalidation that is most hurtful to my spouse is _____ because . . .

- What in my life gets in the way of my efforts to cherish?

Ask your spouse:

- What's one behavior I can eliminate to help you feel more cherished in our marriage?

- Is there something I do that makes it more difficult for you to cherish me?

Establish cherishing attitudes this week:

- Put your trash racks into action. Select one behavior that hinders cherishing in your marriage and do everything you can to eliminate it.

THE CONCEPT

We spend, we save, we
budget and buy.
We splurge on a girl, or we
splurge on a guy.

Pockets, wallets, purses,
and piggy banks—
we work so hard to fill them!

Dollars add up in a long
length of time,
but debts will quickly kill
them.

So we count our coins, we
carry cash,
we sell some stuff and stock
a stash.

But when it's all said and
done, just what does it mean?
We're just a guy and a girl
with some greenbacks between.

THE CONSTİTUENTS

We asked couples, "In your
marriage, who needs financial
security?" Responses:

The Husband: 13%
The Wife: 21%
Both: 67%

Chapter 2

Pursuing Financial Security

Americans are in debt and way out of balance. Specifically it was reported in 2010 that U.S. consumers were $609.8 million in credit card debt. The average credit card debt per household is $14,687. The total U.S. consumer debt is 2.43 trillion. All of these statistics certainly add up to a country obsessed with consumerism but what does that have to do with saving marriages in America.

> Do you wonder if the divorce rate in America would be lower if couples paid down their personal debt and lifted up their marriage vows?

It has everything to do with marriages, because finances are one of the main reasons why couples argue. When I (Dan) was in my twenties, I worked in the money business. As the financial director at a hospital, I oversaw everything about the facility's money, from payroll to purchasing and payables to products. All day long I crunched numbers and made decisions about cash and change. It was all very economic and ego building. I got paid to know about money, and I figured I was pretty good at it.

The story was different back home. Jane was the CFO. After hours of shuffling numbers and calculating rates, I was happy to step aside and just be the CPO—Chief Petty Officer. Yes, that's right. I was known to get very petty over the most insignificant issues.

I felt free to place blame whenever there was a discrepancy in the checkbook. Our positions on the issue were so opposite it was ridiculous.

I was the money man at work, but at home our marriage accounts—financial and beyond—were way out of balance.

The Elephant in the Room

Does anyone see a parallel with divorce rates continuing to be high as well as consumer debt? Do you wonder if the divorce rate in America would be lower if couples paid down their personal debt and lifted up their marriage vows?

In a nationwide survey conducted by two well-known researchers, couples reported that money was the one thing they argued about most—more than careers, kids, communication, chores, and even in-laws. No matter how many candles were on their last anniversary cake, money took the top spot for marital spats.[5] In psychology circles, money is always listed as one of the big three subjects that couples squabble about. These big three can vary depending on which psychologist is speaking, but money is always a member of the trio.

That kind of research isn't exactly earth shattering. Most people are already aware that money is a hot-button issue in marriage.

---

5   S. M. Stanley and H. J. Markman, "Marriage in the 90s: A Nationwide Random Phone Survey" (Denver: PREP, 1997). [Note: In one respondent group (married 32 years plus), "none" was the number-one answer to "Name the one thing that you and your partner argue about most," with more than 40 percent of respondents choosing "none." In this same group, "money" was the next common response to "none." For all five of the other groups, "money" was the number-one answer by a nearly 10-point-percentage margin or more in all groups.]

Income brackets aside, very few husbands and wives say, "We totally agree on finances" or "Finances are really not an issue for us." Nope, in pretty much every marriage, money can make the two spouses want to pull their own hair out. Disagreements about money show up on all social levels and all economic tiers—it doesn't matter if a couple is rolling in the dough or scraping the bottom of the barrel.

Spenders marry savers and savers marry spenders. Penny-pinchers try to make it with budget breakers. Financial planners try to build portfolios with impulse buyers. Mrs. X, who line-items everything, is paired with Mr. X, who loses all the credit card receipts. Mr. Z grew up eating five dinners a week at restaurants, but his wife expects the inexpensive homemade meals she was raised on. And undoubtedly, the guy who won't spend twenty bucks on a pair of shoes is hitched to the woman who could easily spend two hundred dollars on glorified flip-flops.

> Certain issues transcend gender. Money doesn't appear to be one of them.

It's as common as dirt to have problems like these. Financial differences are practically a given in marriage. They're bound to happen because money is a necessity and because it's important to people. However, when it comes to finances, there's one common problem that most couples in America fail to identify in their marriages. They get stuck in their struggles—the saver/spender problem or the pinching/breaking issue—and they miss what's really going on. They fight about the right price of shoes, but they never get around to recognizing the elephant in the room: They're not pursuing financial security together.

The Chromosome Factor

Certain issues transcend gender. Money doesn't appear to be one of them. In fact, a strong case can be made that certain generalizations apply to men and money and to women and money. As a general rule, men and women approach finances from two separate angles, and it all starts with grammar.

That's right—grammar. Now, before you throw this book down in a flashback to eighth-grade English and three months of diagramming sentences, read on.

"Financial security" is what we call it, on both sides of the gender gap. The terminology is the same no matter how many X chromosomes you have. But the definition of that term is completely different for most women than it is for most men. Financial security to a wife is normally nothing like what financial security is to her husband.

Dr. Peter: Financial Conflict

If I had to classify the couples I see on a professional basis, I would assert that nearly 90 percent of them have financial dysfunctions to work through. These issues run the gamut, covering a wide range of issues including:

- Communication about finances
- Money management
- Trust with money and financial decisions
- Goals or priorities within finances
- Money's impact on stress in a marriage
- Handling conflicts about finances
- Issues that stem from families of origin

The Husband's World

To most men, financial security is a verb. It's something they do, an action they perform. The emphasis is on securing. Financial security is an accomplishment a man can reach. A man's sense of financial well-being comes from acquiring, gaining, obtaining, and having money or material possessions.

Research shows that men generally have a provider mentality; they want to take care of their family's essential financial needs. They want to make enough money to sustain the family bank accounts, balance the checkbooks, and pay that monthly electric bill. They want to put food on tables, vehicles in garages, clothes on backs, and family members in homes. In the very best sense, they desire power and influence as far as money is concerned.

For a typical husband, this means he prefers that his wife does not have to work. Even though a second income is beneficial in taking some of the load off his shoulders, there is a part of that load he wants to carry. He wants his income to cover his family's necessities.

Because financial security is something a man *does,* a husband often views his family's financial status as a reflection of his ability to provide. This is crucial for women to understand. A sizable amount of a man's personal esteem comes from acquiring money well—gaining, obtaining, and having enough for his family to be (from his point of view) comfortable. A man's income bracket can deeply affect his picture of himself, and so it is often through financial gain that a husband seeks to build his self-image.

Perhaps because it's the ultimate sign of being able to provide enough, men like to have stuff that goes above and beyond necessities. This is where convertibles, fancy gadgets, big-screen TVs, and sports equipment come in. A man revels in these things because they're more than just toys to him. They're security.

The Wife's World

Financial security to most women is a noun. It's something they feel, a state of existence they can experience. A woman's sense of financial well-being comes from knowing, believing, feeling, and trusting that she will be OK when it comes to money and material possessions. Financial security is comfort she can wrap around herself. The emphasis is on stability.

On the female side of a marriage relationship, there is usually little or no desire to be the primary provider in a home. Instead, most women like to have a choice whether to work outside the home. If they choose to work, that's great, but they don't like to *have* to work.

A wife wants to know there's enough money to get by on, but normally she doesn't want to be the one depended on to earn that all-important "enough." Even well-educated, high-earning women don't like to feel the stress of being the breadwinner. They don't enjoy being responsible to provide for their family's day-to-day financial support.

When a woman is working outside the home, it's normally her preference to spend her earnings on life's nonessentials. It's optimal if she can contribute little comforts for herself and her family. This is where home decor, special outings, and six different pairs of black shoes come into the picture.

Alongside multiple other variables, finances serve to make a woman feel settled into and prepared for her life. She relishes stability and dependability in money matters, and she often doesn't feel stable if she has to depend on herself to supply all the cash. This issue is of utmost importance to a woman. In fact, among unmarried women and single mothers, arguably the most overwhelming aspect of life is the continuous demand to provide funds. Of all the stresses they face, financial strain is the stress they feel most acutely.

Although many women enjoy contributing to the family finances, they often don't want to feel responsible to make the necessary funds available. In this sense, many women *do* marry for money—or, more specifically, for the stability that comes with money. In marriage, a wife desires a partnership that will sustain day-to-day living. When she has a spouse who's dependable in providing the resources, she feels security for herself and for her children. (Typically, the more children a woman has, the greater need she feels to experience security in this area of life.)

In no way does any of this mean that women are gold diggers, money hungry, or insincere when they tie the knot. It simply means financial security is a big deal for women, big enough to have a big effect on their sense of well-being. It's vital for a wife, especially if she is a mother, to know that her husband is her comrade in the battle of finances. In the words of one working woman, "It's not about amounts or figures; it's about togetherness. If I didn't have my husband, I would feel I couldn't survive financially. But with him, I'm sure we can make it."

As with any generalization, of course there are exceptions. There are men who don't have much of a provider mentality, and there are women who like to be the family breadwinner. In your marriage, the phenomenon might be flip-flopped.

Still, most married couples in America can easily relate to the noun/verb phenomenon, and most couples understand how frustrating it can

The Noun/Verb Phenomenon

Husband:	**Wife:**
Financial security is something I do.	Financial security is something I feel.
It's about providing what's needed	It's about feeling cared for.
Finances are commodities to be secured.	Finances are instruments that affect stability.
It's an esteem issue.	It's a surety issue.
I want to make enough for my family.	I want my family to be OK.
I'm seeking security with myself.	I'm seeking security with my situation.
Security is built through gain.	Security is built through constancy.
I want to provide the basics.	I want to provide extras.
I like to have extras.	I like to have the basics.

be. While the husband looks to seize financial security, the wife seeks to wrap herself up in it. He's trying to overflow the piggy bank; she's trying to make it a pig in a blanket. The husband wonders why his wife cures relational stress by shopping. The wife wonders why her husband always wants a bigger TV. The man works toward esteem and the woman works toward security. The man chases cash and the

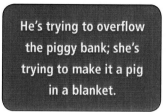

He's trying to overflow the piggy bank; she's trying to make it a pig in a blanket.

woman chases comfort, and usually neither party catches anything but an attitude about how their spouse can be so unfeeling about money.

Which One Rules?

The thing that really stinks about our financial differences is that in marriage they naturally turn us away from our spouse. Lost in their own grammar worlds, husbands and wives pursue financial security as individuals rather than as couples. And because they're both seeking very different versions of security, their efforts divide them.

Instead of building common ground and making their money work for both of them, the two spouses keep their efforts separate, like his-and-hers towels. Rather than making their finances a marriage-centered issue, the couple keeps things self-centered. And eventually they sort of hang each other out to dry as everything begins to unravel.

What we often miss when pursuing individual financial security is that our own personal desires have a distinct way of stomping all over our spouse's. The husband works for raises and big-ticket items because he gets esteem from those things, but, in the meantime, the wife often gets the impression he doesn't care about family stability, which is most essential to her. Or she spends money on a "luxury" item because doing so makes her feel secure, but as a result, he often gets the impression she is careless about necessities, which are so important to him. Even

Income versus Expenses

Many couples have no idea whether they earn more than they spend or spend more than they earn. Which category describes your marriage? To figure this out, calculate the following:

_____   *Income per month*
            salary, interest, dividends, other

Subtract the following expenses:
_____   *Charitable Gifts*
            tithe, sponsorships, gifts to nonprofits
_____   *Housing*
            mortgage/rent, insurance, taxes, utilities, repairs
_____   *Food*
_____   *Vehicles*
            payments, fuel, insurance, repairs
_____   *Insurance*
            life, medical, other
_____   *Debts*
            credit card, loans
_____   *Recreation*
            activities, movie rental, eating out, vacation
_____   *Clothing*
_____   *Savings*
_____   *Medical*
            doctor, dentist, prescriptions, etc.
_____   *School/Childcare*
            tuition, materials, etc.
_____   *Miscellaneous*
            anything that doesn't work in another category
_____   *Calculate Total Expenses*

Gross Income   _____
Less Expenses   _____
Final Figure*   _____

If your final figure is a negative number, you're spending more than you earn. This is not the road to financial security.

when neither spouse intends to offend the other, matrimonial finances cause them to rub each other the wrong way and they end up having to massage each other's ego. It's great for men and women to pursue financial security. It's vital, really. But in marriage, it's not enough. Building an extraordinary marriage means moving beyond ordinary in the area of financial security. And that's a security that serves as a benefit to the marriage, first and foremost.

Are your financial decisions making your marriage better? If your answer is no, then it's time for you and your spouse

> The marriage should rule the money, not vice versa.

to start molding a financial security that's more marriage centered. It's time to learn a new mantra. Let's all say it together: *Our marriage is more important than our money.* The marriage takes precedence here, which means the marriage should rule the money, not vice versa.

If you take the time to browse through a few books about money management, you'll quickly find that most leading experts on finances advocate the same types of things. They'll give you advice on saving money, avoiding debt, and planning for retirement. These are all very good habits to practice. (We recommend that every couple reads a good budget guide or two.) We're not going to pretend that we're gurus when it comes to financial planning, but we do have helpful suggestions on how you can let your money work on behalf of your relationship. Try some of these:

Hold Hands

The next time you get into a disagreement about money (assuming that happens sometimes), don't let it blow up in your face. Go for a walk together or sit across from each other to talk, but whatever you do, hold hands. Let it be a visible reminder to you both that the marriage is more important than the money—you'll be surprised at how far this one takes you!

Compliment Each Other's Efforts

Notice the things your husband or wife does to alleviate some of the stress on your finances. Has she been clipping coupons and shopping sales to save on spending? Or did he pick up overtime last week? Has she been putting off buying something she really wants because it's not *really* a necessity? Is he always faithful in providing an income?

If so, make sure you express your appreciation. Give him a big hug and tell him you've noticed. Tell her you love her for helping to carry financial burdens. Just for fun, be over the top with your gratitude—speak in exclamation points, and watch as your spouse's confidence soars.

Determine Your "Talking Number"

Between the two of you, decide on an amount of money neither spouse should spend without discussing it first. This is a great way to promote unity while also providing freedom. If a couple decides that twenty dollars a week can be freebie money for each, then the husband can splurge on Starbucks a few times and the wife can buy a new DVD. Both have financial liberty, but it exists under the umbrella of unity—if either person wants to buy an item for more than twenty dollars, both have to agree first.

Set Generosity Goals

Choose a charity, a family, or a program that could benefit from your financial contribution. (Or choose several if you can.) As a couple, discuss giving and set a goal for yourselves: How much can you offer to a person or group in need? How much can you play a role in fighting poverty, hardship, AIDS, famine? How much can you help children, families, single moms, elderly people? What extras could you sacrifice for a month or a year in order to make an impact?

When your money is more than just a cash cow for *me, me, me* or *us, us, us,* you'll have a much more healthy perspective, which can only help your marriage and other relationships.

Create a Refuge

No, not a refuge *away from* your money but a refuge *within* it. Is there an issue or pattern in your finances that continually threatens your marriage? If so, do whatever you can to resolve it. Create financial security in every way you can. See a financial planner. Cut up the credit cards. Downsize to a smaller house, a smaller car. Say no to friends who pressure you to lead a more extravagant lifestyle than you can afford. Commit to valuing your relationship above the other extras.

Avoiding a Wedge

"The love of money is a root of all kinds of evil."[6] The love of money is also a root of all kinds of divorces. Not only are finances one of the big three bickering points for couples, but disagreements about money also serve as one of the most common reasons for the dissolution of marriages. In fact, in a recent landmark survey, 43 percent of people who had been divorced indicated that financial problems contributed to their divorce.[7]

When spouses don't actively work to make the marriage the priority over money, it's very easy for finances to take over completely. That's why, for far too many couples, money rules the roost. Observing their everyday behavior makes that fact clear. The two spouses keep things harshly unbalanced (for example, one spouse makes all the financial decisions; the other makes none) or obsessively even ("You spent fifty dollars; I'm gonna spend fifty dollars too"). They make snide remarks about each other's spending habits. They hoard money or bitterly keep things separate—"I earned all of this, so you don't get to spend

---

6 1 Timothy 6:10a HCSB.

7 C. Johnson, S. Stanley, N. Glenn, P. Amato, S. Nock, H. Markman, and M. Dion, "Marriage in Oklahoma: 2001 Baseline Statewide Survey on Marriage and Divorce," a project of the Oklahoma Marriage Initiative with Oklahoma State University's Bureau for Social Research (p. 15).

any of it." They hide purchases or lie about how much money they're spending. By no means are their actions with finances determined by what benefits the marriage. Instead, it's all about the money.

> The love of money is also a root of all kinds of divorces.

When a husband and wife aren't working to keep money secondary, they've often unwittingly allowed it to become primary. And there's a big problem with that. If money is primary in a marriage, there's no doubt it's slowly tearing the two spouses apart. Think about it:

- When you disagree about money matters, do you resolve the conflict in a way that reduces stress and arguments?
- Do your financial priorities foster unity and bring you closer together?
- Do your spending habits promote honesty between the two of you?
- Do you each show appreciation for the contributions that your spouse brings to the finances (through income, saving, etc.)?
- Are you adequately preparing for your future together (children, medical expenses, emergencies, retirement)?
- Do you challenge each other to be less selfish and more giving with money?
- Do your financial habits reflect both of your individual needs for security?

If you're answering no to any of these questions, take it as a sign that money is creating weak spots at places in your marriage. "Where your treasure is, there your heart will be also,"[8] advises the New Testament. In other words, our behavior expresses our loyalty in boldface. That's why it's so crucial for spouses to actively pursue financial security for *their marriage*. Every other pursuit creates instability between the husband and the wife. Always choose the relationship over the cash. After all, what person wants to play second fiddle to a bank account?

8 Matthew 6:21 HCSB.

Chapter 2 Follow-up
Pursuing Financial Security

His & Hers:

Rate the following 1 to 10 in order of importance (1 = most important), then compare your answers.

His	Hers	
_____	_____	Saving for our retirement
_____	_____	Owning expensive things
_____	_____	Sticking to a predetermined budget
_____	_____	Putting kids through college
_____	_____	Having an emergency savings supply
_____	_____	Paying off our debt
_____	_____	Owning/upgrading our home
_____	_____	Having as much as/more than someone else
_____	_____	Going on nice vacations
_____	_____	Buying our "dream splurge" purchases

Answer the following individually, then discuss:

- How would you describe your financial skill level and knowledge?

- What does financial security look like to you?

- How much is "enough"?

- What is your biggest frustration in the area of finances?

Ask your spouse:

- Is the noun/verb phenomenon true in our marriage? If so, how? If not, how are we different?

- How often do we have conflict about money in our marriage? Are there any patterns to these conflicts? What do those patterns suggest about our relationship?

- How did your family of origin deal with financial matters?

- Are we in trouble financially? If so, what is a helpful change that we can make immediately?

Pursuing financial security this week:

- Together decide on one financial goal that's important to both of you. Make a plan to achieve your goal and take your first steps in that direction.

THE CONCEPT

Sex is a big deal. A really big deal.

Marriage is designed for one man and one woman. Sex is designed for one man and one woman. In your marriage, you are either that one man or that one woman. You are the only person your spouse can rightfully look to for sexual satisfaction. Are you doing your best to fulfill that role? It requires thoughtfulness, creativity, honesty, conversation, and flexibility. Do all you can to keep each other happy in the bedroom.

THE CONSTİTUENTS

We asked couples, "In your marriage, who's more interested in sex?" Responses:

The Husband: 64%
The Wife: 9%
Both: 27%

Chapter 3

Discovering Sexual Satisfaction

The sexual revolution, which began in the 60s, has permeated just about every area of American life. A rise in teenage pregnancy, sexually-transmitted infections and diseases, as well as complications with emotional connectedness has all resulted from a far-too-casual attitude about a very intimate act.

Marriage in America has not escaped the effects of the sexual revolution. In fact, marriages may be suffering even more so from the laid-back response to the idea that sex is no longer just reserved for the marriage bed. A little sexual freedom has probably led to a lot of extra-marital affairs, but what is more disconcerting is that sexual satisfaction between married couples has declined simply due to today's more unrealistic expectations and views about sex. The advent of the Internet and rampant pornography, instant messaging, and texting on cell phones has done nothing but muddy the sexual waters where people are already drowning in confusion and helplessness.

Americans are far too eager to talk about sex in magazine articles, on talk shows, reality television, and through media outlets such as; YouTube, Facebook and Twitter resulting in couples comparing their sex lives with strangers. It's hard not to strain your ears to hear the TV when you hear a married couple talking about sex. It's a natural curiosity.

Sexual satisfaction is not necessarily about the number of times a couple has sex but about the quality of their sexual experience. In this chapter we explore the many differences between a man and woman's view on sex and give you practical ideas on what you can do to increase the sexual satisfaction in your marriage.

In this chapter, we will discuss sexpectations, sacrifice, cannonballs, and how God views sex. If we are going to stay married for life, we can't ignore a very real problem that prevents couples from reaching the pinnacle in their marriage and that's sexual satisfaction.

Starting Out

It was mid-December, and I (Dan) was Christmas shopping with Jane at a local mall. We were almost finished buying presents for the kids when we walked past a lingerie store. Jane stopped suddenly and said, "Honey, I need some perfume. Could we stop in here for a minute?"

I'm convinced that walking through negligee displays is one of the most intimidating things a man can do in his entire life. We can barely handle the stress of it; we're hands-in-the-pockets-and-eyes-to-the-floor nervous the whole time. This particular day was no different for me—in the beginning, that is. I stood beside Jane while she browsed the perfumes, doing my best to avoid eye contact with anyone and everyone in the store. Then, all of a sudden, it dawned on me: I was a married man out shopping with my wife, whom I love. Of all the guys who walk into lingerie stores, *I* was totally legal.

A slight grin spread across my face. With newfound confidence, I lifted my chin to glance around a bit.

That was when I saw it. The outfit was displayed on a mannequin in the corner of the store, lacy and black and with a garter belt to boot.

Va-va-*voom*.

"Honey," I said, with an impish nod toward the outfit. "Look over there."

Jane turned to look, then she looked back at me. The expression on her face was practical, logical. She shook her head.

"Dan," she said, "my *grandma* used to wear that."

You put that outfit on, I thought, *and I'll call you "Granny" or anything else you want me to call you.*

For a few seconds, Jane's face flashed a look that said, *I don't have time for your nonsense.* "C'mon," she prodded, moving toward the checkout. "Let's buy the perfume and finish shopping."

For the first five or six years of our marriage, Jane and I had problems in our sexual relationship. Big problems. But if you would have asked her about it back then, she probably would have told you everything was fine between us. She honestly thought it was.

In her defense, I hadn't told her much of anything about the struggles I was having within our sex life. I hadn't told her that I was convinced the numbers were way off—that I wanted sex a whole lot more than she did. I hadn't told her about the nights I stayed awake, upset that she could sleep so peacefully when I was all hot and bothered. I hadn't told her there wasn't enough creativity for me.

I hadn't told her that our predictable sexual relationship had become mundane for me. It was nice to have sex on Tuesday and Thursday at 9:27, but after a year or so, my excitement for that schedule had left completely. I hadn't told her that a woman at work had boldly propositioned me one day and that for a split second it had been an acute temptation. I hadn't told her about how much I struggled with lust. I hadn't told her anything that would have let her know that everything wasn't fine.

But then one night we had a conversation that changed our marriage. The magnitude of that one night was too huge to adequately describe on paper. I told her everything. It changed everything. It meant the world to me. It meant the world to our marriage. And it meant the world to Jane, whom I had kept in the dark for so long.

Which brings me back to the lingerie store that day at the mall. My wife was headed toward the sales counter with her perfume in hand when she glanced back and saw a pleading smirk on my face. She stopped, turned, and gave the outfit a second look.

As they say, the rest is history. I don't believe in Santa Claus, but Saint Nick's grandma definitely paid a visit on Christmas Eve.

The Tricky Part

Perhaps it would be good for us to note here that chapter 3 in this book isn't merely about *sex*. Married people in America are having sex every day, but not necessarily satisfying sex. Chapter 3 is about *sexual satisfaction*. There's a huge difference.

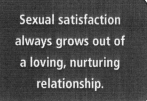

Sexual satisfaction always grows out of a loving, nurturing relationship.

Just about anybody can have sex. It doesn't take any skill beyond the ability to survive puberty. Sexual satisfaction, on the other hand, requires talent and expertise—a keen eye, an aware mind, and, we dare say, the moves of a master! Sex has many versions—from beautiful and pure to (sadly) distorted and perverse. But sexual satisfaction always grows out of a loving, nurturing relationship. Sex is limited to biology, contact, climax, and body fluids. Sexual satisfaction is worlds bigger and worlds better than that.

But sexual satisfaction is also not easy to achieve.

The tricky thing about sexual satisfaction is that it's different for each couple and depends on many variables, including the spouses' ages, how long they've been married, the combined force of their sex drives, their moods, recent amount of stress, their health, and whether the kids sleep soundly at night. These and any number of other factors are the undertones that direct an individual couple as they define sexual satisfaction in their marriage.

And then there's a host of other complications. Body image can make people incredibly uncomfortable during sex or prevent them from even wanting sex. This is definitely a problem in America where obesity is prevalent. Not to mention the onslaught of magazines, movies, and television shows that insist on bringing people distorted views of body image. Intercourse itself can be painful. Abusive experiences can distort the way we view sexuality. Stringent religious upbringings can make sex seem evil. Prior sexual relationships can warp the way couples relate. Promiscuity can make married sex feel shameful or even boring. Pregnancies and births can change everything.

So it's a loaded issue to begin with that dumps out into so many other areas of a person's life, but there's still one more thing that serves as a barrier to sexual satisfaction in a marriage. On top of everything else, there is this: When it comes to sexuality, men and women live in two totally separate worlds. Sometimes they can barely even begin to relate to each other. You want extremes? You've got 'em.

A Litmus Test

Most psychologists will tell you that, generally speaking, a woman's sexuality revolves around relational components, while a man's sexuality is dominated by all things physical. A man's body is his primary motivator toward sex; a woman is driven toward sex primarily by her feelings and emotions. It can take hours for the wife's mood to work up to a point where she'll be eager for a good romp in the bedroom. Give the husband about three seconds of nudity (make that one second . . . OK, a nanosecond), and he's ready to go.

From the very beginning of a marriage, it's like this. In fact, a husband and wife alone on their wedding night are a pretty good litmus test as to how differently men and women approach sex. Picture it: Upon entering their honeymoon suite (or the back of their limo or a broom closet at the reception—don't think it hasn't been done), these two lovers have the same thing in mind, but in two totally dissimilar ways.

The new bride is concerned about choosing just the right lighting for their time together, not to mention the perfect negligee and a redo of her hair and makeup. She's thinking about caresses and sweet nothings, lace and rose petals, perfumes and soft music, luxurious massages, and chocolate. She definitely has sex on the brain.

So does the groom. He wants to hang the "Do Not Disturb" sign, throw back the sheets, and get naked.

It's likely that all of us have observed the vast differences between the ways men and women are wired. It's true that our approaches to sex can create some hilariously awkward moments between husbands and wives. But it's also true that our approaches to sex create moments and situations that aren't funny at all.

There's the wife who resents when her husband wants sex in the middle of an unresolved argument or the middle of the night. There's the husband who resents the fact that an argument with his wife about dishwasher detergent can hit the pause button on their sex life instead of rev it up. There's the couple for whom sex doesn't rank above number eighty-three on *his* priority list for the day, but *she's* trying to initiate a little get-together. Or he's dying to install fluorescent lighting in their bedroom, while she continues to turn off more than just lights. It almost seems like a cruel joke, doesn't it? He can't relate to her desires; she can't relate to his. Their confusions and misunderstandings pile up until the load becomes too heavy to bear. Intimacy fades, sex becomes leverage in the relationship, and everybody is singing, *"I can't get no . . . satisfaction."*

So we're left with this: If a husband and wife define sexual satisfaction by two completely opposite terms, how can they ever begin to hope their marriage will be sexually satisfying?

Sexpectations

Both men and women have high expectations when it comes to sex (*sexpectations,* you could call them). But in most marriages,

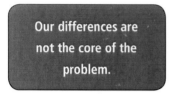

what the husband expects sexually is nothing like what the wife expects. For many couples, the troubles and the arguments begin and end right there. Still, although our inherent differences definitely help to make sex a major

marital contention point, we shouldn't get hung up on that fact alone. Our differences are not the core of the problem.

The biggest hurdle on the road toward sexual satisfaction isn't a matter of hormones, chromosomes, or body parts. Our biggest hurdle is

Her Terms	His Terms
I'm not really in the mood right now.	What's mood got to do with anything?
We haven't spent time together all week, and I'm expected to want sex?	We haven't spent much time together this week. How about we have sex now?
If you attend to my emotions, we can have sex more often.	If we have sex more often, I'll be much more attentive.
Honey, I'm plumb exhausted tonight.	You're tired? No problem; this shouldn't take long.
I'd like to feel sexy when I'm with you.	I'd like to have sex with you.
This marriage is about more than only sex, you know.	What's the point of being married if you don't have sex?

not *him, him, him* or *her, her, her*. It's the battle hymn of our own republic because we are usually singing all about *me, me, me*. In pursuing a sexual relationship, we hold very little or no regard for our spouse's sexuality.

Whether we state our demands verbally or not, in the sexual category of a marriage relationship, most of us have very clear terms. Let's look at a few classic examples:

On his terms, sex is about sex. On her terms, sex is about sex, moods, emotions, and everything else. On his terms, sex should happen more often. On her terms, it happens often enough. Or vice versa. (Without fail, that one guy out of a thousand who doesn't have a strong sex drive marries a woman who does.)

It seems that nearly every couple faces *term limits* when it comes to defining the parameters of their sex life. Still, the real problem here is not the terms or the fact that they're different. The real problem is that in most marriages, both spouses stand firm on the terms instead of offering flex-ability on their sex-ability.

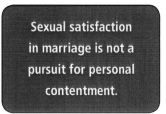

Sexual satisfaction in marriage is not a pursuit for personal contentment. This isn't something you get an individual medal for; this is a team sport. And to play well—to *win*—together in this area of your marriage, you have to discover a sex life that capitalizes on the strengths both of you bring to it.

The Bedroom and the Big Top

Husbands, this starts with us. Let's all begin by raising our right hands and acknowledging that, for the most part, we're clueless about women. Now, with that in mind, let's do some investigating.

One of the most important steps toward sexual satisfaction in your marriage is understanding that sexuality is a *part* of your wife's identity.

A part—just as her shoes, her job, her cooking skills, her family of origin, and her favorite color of nail polish are all parts of her identity. Your wife's sexuality helps to define her, but in her mind it's just one of the hundreds of things that help to form the kaleidoscope of who she is.

Not only that, but a woman's sexuality is strongly linked to nearly everything else in her life. In other words, circumstances and events that seem to have absolutely nothing to do with sex might have everything to do with your wife's sex drive. Finishing a project at work or even having a good hair day can make her feel incredibly sexy, but if she's having problems with a close friend, she's not as likely to be in the mood. If the kids behaved like cherubs all day? Feelin' sexy. If the two of you argued six hours ago? Maybe not so sexy. If it's a good hair day *and* there was an argument six hours ago? It might be worth a shot!

When your wife is feeling anxious or pressured, it's very common for her libido to be significantly lower than it is when she's relaxed and hassle free. This happens because the female mind views sex as an emotionally-based activity that culminates with a sex act. (Read that again: The female mind views sex as an emotionally- based activity that culminates with a sex act.) If her emotions are strained or drained, her sex drive will be lame. For a woman, sexuality doesn't revolve around only physical things. As far as she's concerned, there's much more to it, and we're not talking merely about foreplay.

It's probable that your wife craves sensuality more than she craves sex. For her, feeling sensual can be much more dynamic than the act of intercourse itself. In fact, the sensation she experiences when she knows you desire her likely means more to her than even the most intense orgasm.

It's incredibly meaningful for your wife to know that you're in this for her, not just for her body. Although grabbing at her breast or backside might seem like the ideal mode of foreplay to you, they might leave her feeling cheapened, as if she's nothing more than a sex object. However, when she feels you've appreciated and affirmed her emotionally, she feels closer to you and sexier than ever.

Still, that's not to say the physical side of all this should be forgotten. Most women relish the emotional connection they share with their spouses, and they also deeply value the experience of sex and sexual climax. (And she might even be able to climax two or three times to your once!) However, on average it takes a woman much longer to work up to orgasm than it does a man.

If sexual performances were circus events, you, the husband, would be the human cannonball. Climb in, light the fuse, there's a big bang and a cloud of smoke, and you're all done. The crowd cheers. You are the human cannonball at its finest. Your wife, on the other hand, is not. In this show, she's more like a trapeze artist. Her outfit is sexier, her act is just as thrilling, but it's on a much more gradual schedule and takes longer to work up to the big finish.

Bringing your wife to orgasm is an art. What works some days might not work other days. Sometimes it requires a lot of focused effort, and other times it happens without a hitch. But if you roll over and fall asleep as soon as you've climaxed, you're giving her the impression that intercourse is all for *you.* Your wife is likely to feel tossed aside like a piece of trash while you drift into dreamy land.

Husbands, living for something bigger in the sexual climate of your marriage means living with consideration for your wife's sexuality. When you figure this out, it will make a world of difference in your relationship. Your wife already has it figured out; she's just waiting for you to read this!

How can you consider your wife's sexuality? A few ways are:

- *Acknowledge the qualities that make her special to you.* Let her know you respect her character and that you're impressed with her concern for others. Tell her how beautiful she is and that you love her sense of style. Show interest in her goals; encourage her in her hobbies.

- *Recognize when it's not the right moment.* Be sensitive to the times when she's tired, anxious, or upset, and understand that stress can make it difficult for her to switch gears and get in the mood. Show her you care by taking the kids off her hands for a few hours, giving her a back rub, or picking up the vacuum.
- *Consider her timetable.* Be mindful of the way your wife's body works and work your hardest to pleasure your wife physically. Ask her what she likes and what she doesn't like. Consider having a warm-up or a cool-down phase of your sexual aerobics. Kiss her. Caress her. Talk or hold each other for a while if that's what she enjoys. Remember that sex is for both of you.
- *Emphasize the love and connection you share.* Send her flowers or leave a note on the bathroom mirror. Tell her you love her. Hold her. Dance with her. Learn to enjoy the depth that an emotional bond can bring to your sexual relationship; it will mean the world to your wife.

Cannonball to the Rescue

Of all the things there are to say about sex, intimacy, and making love, there's one key thing for women to understand. Ironically, it's also the one thing most wives wouldn't naturally know on their own and the one thing most husbands are afraid to admit. Are you ready for this? If you want to live for something bigger in your marriage—if you want to love your husband with a selfless love—then it's important for you to understand that sex is a big deal to him. A very big deal. You might have to think outside the box on this one—way outside. In fact, let's just get rid of the box, OK?

As we've already discussed, sexuality is a *part* of a woman's identity. We'll use nearly the same statement in speaking to wives; however, in this case the emphasis changes greatly. Watch the italics here: Sexuality is a part of a man's *identity*.

Your husband's sexuality plays a huge part in the way he defines himself as a man and as a husband. If he feels accepted and desired as your lover, his self-image swells to massive proportions. He feels happy, confident, strong, capable, and wanted. He is Superhubby to the rescue. On the other hand, if he feels rejected or unwanted as your lover, his self-image deflates along with other parts of his body. He feels dissatisfied and insecure, demoralized and inadequate, shunned.

Equally damaging is the behavior of a wife who complies with her husband's desires but does so reluctantly. During a national broadcast talk show a woman confessed that she regularly watches TV while her husband had sex with her (if that could indeed be called sex *with* her). From a man's perspective, a wife who's not mentally in the game, might as well forfeit than attempt to play. It communicates that she doesn't enjoy being intimate with him. Being sexually available is not the issue here; a man wants a wife who is sexually engaged.

For the sake of comparison, consider this: A man longs to feel sexual to the same degree that most women long to feel beautiful. It's *that* important to us. So when a wife says no to her husband's sexual advances (including the classic "Honey, I have a headache"), no isn't the only thing a husband is inclined to hear. Instead, the messages he gets are "I don't want to be intimate with you," "You're not attractive to me," and "You don't mean much to me." As we've already discussed, communications like that (even when they're completely unintended) are massive blows. From the husband's perspective, *N–O* is a loaded response, and when it's fired, it carries a crushing force.

And one more factor plays into all of this: On average, men desire sex and think about sex much more often than women do. Some studies have even suggested men think about sex once every forty-five seconds. Compared to blinking, that means he blinks only nine times for every time he thinks about sex.[9] Since a man becomes aroused by visual images (and there are suggestive ones all around) and since his body is buzzing with testosterone (the hormone that drives people sexually), it should come as no surprise that sex is on his mind often. The desire doesn't seem to diminish much with age either. Men in their sixties and seventies are as enticed with sex as they were in their twenties. When it comes to sexual frequency, we're all practically robots.

It's physically impossible for your husband to completely suppress his desire for intimacy; his body simply won't let him forget about it. We won't claim that sex is a *need* for a man, but we can tell you that sometimes it definitely feels that way. And the husband who is repeatedly denied sexual release often begrudges his wife for the displeasure he feels sexually.

Wives, living for something bigger in the sexual climate of your marriage means living with consideration for your husband's sexuality. How can you do this? Here are a few ways:

- ***Know that your husband isn't perverted.*** If he wants sex more often (even *much* more often) than you do, that doesn't mean he's obsessed. Scolding him for having a strong sex drive is not only hurtful; it also makes about as much sense as scolding him for having feet. Acknowledge the intensity of his sex drive and the impact it has on his life, and enjoy the fact that he is sexually interested in you.

- ***Avoid "No" at all costs.*** By no means should you feel pressure to cater to your husband's every whim and fantasy. But if there's a situation when he's interested, but the timing is poor for you, it's best to suggest a later time slot for intimacy. Try "Can it wait an hour?" or "How about tomorrow?" or even "I can be ready in fifteen

---

9   We wonder if those researchers actually meant every four to five seconds, which would figure to be about one sexual thought for every blink. Sometimes that seems more accurate.

Dr. Peter on Visual Images

The Internet is having a major effect on marriages.

According to a *Time* magazine article, there are 260 million pages of pornography online. This is an increase of 1,800 percent since 1998. Pornography accounts for 7 percent of the 3.3 billion Web pages indexed by Google.

My own experience as a Christian counselor and the conversations I have had with many of you suggest a dramatic increase in the number of couples with problems in their marriages because of the husband's use of Internet pornography.

Studies have shown that men who frequently look at pornography:

- May develop unrealistic expectations of women's appearance and
- behavior (including sexual behavior)
- Have difficulty forming and sustaining relationships
- Have trouble feeling sexually satisfied

Considering these problems that come from pornography along with many others, I encourage any individual or couples who have experienced this problem not to lose hope.

I have seen many individuals and couples heal and transform their lives after negative effects have taken their toll. So reach out for help and try to get healing.

minutes." That way, your husband knows you're still interested in being intimate with him, but he gets the message that *right now* isn't exactly the right time.

- *Play.* Appreciate the enticing quality of sex in your marriage. Buy a new nightie (the shorter the better) and stash it in your husband's drawer along with a note that says "How 'bout it?" Plant Polaroid pictures of yourself where he (and only he) will see them. Send him an e-mail to say you've got the whole evening free and you're all his.

God and Sex

One thing that really bothers us is that many people seem to think God wants us to have nothing to do with sex. That's crazy! Why would God create something good for us and then not want us enjoy it. To these folks, sex is something dirty, a forbidden topic—the one evil indulgence God lets people get away with. To them it's as far removed from spirituality as they can possibly get.

With all due respect, these people are way off base. The confusion may stem from the fact that many people in America tend to associate sex with just love and God created it for love in the context of marriage. Its design is not to be something that causes wounds, resentment, or separation in a relationship. Rather, God's intent for sex is that it should bring a couple together.

God's Word doesn't ignore or tiptoe around the topic of sex. Instead, the Bible openly kicks up its heels in tribute to marital sex. "[T]ake pleasure in the wife of your youth," and "[L]et her breasts always satisfy you; be lost in her love forever."[1] The book of Hebrews, in advising against adultery, states that marriage (and, by inference, the marriage bed) deserves to "be respected by all."[2] Song of Songs alone comprises 117 verses of erotic poetry, including these gems:

"Take me with you—let us hurry."[3]

"Your stature is like a palm tree. . . I said, 'I will climb the palm tree/and take hold of its fruit.'"[4]

"His mouth is sweetness. / He is absolutely desirable."[5]

"I have taken off my clothing." / How can I put it back on?"[6]

(Want to memorize Scripture? How 'bout those for a start?)

---

1 Proverbs 5:18b and 19b NIV.
2 Hebrews 13:4a NIV.
3 Song of Songs 1:4a NIV.
4 Song of Songs 7:7a and 8a NIV.
5 Song of Songs 5:16a NIV.
6 Song of Songs 5:3a NIV.

- *Make the first move.* Show your husband that you're interested in him sexually. (We have yet to meet a man who doesn't *love* it when his wife initiates intimacy.) Learn to view intimacy and your body as important gifts you can offer to him. Enjoy your role as the *only* woman who holds the license to be his lover. Take pride in that role and uphold its significance in your marriage. It'll wow your husband's socks off.

Sacrifice and Selflessness

Used properly, sex is an incredible force toward the positive within a marriage. It's a natural adhesive that helps to hold two people together. Sex creates a world in which only the two exist, a place reserved for husband and wife alone. It connects a husband and wife physically and emotionally, so they feel united both in body and in spirit. This unique bond is so powerful it has a way of smoothing out rough areas in a marriage. It can solve arguments and dissolve disagreements in the amount of time it takes to dance the tango nude. And that's a really good thing. (The smoothing effect, we mean. Depending on your dance skills, the naked tango can be dangerous.)

Still, of all the steps in this book, this is by far one of the most difficult. Not only is it deeply personal with the potential to be very complicated and confusing, but the process of discovering sexual satisfaction is also always changing and adapting in marriage. It can improve with age, but it remains a fascinating, unique, never-ending process of learning. As long as you and your spouse are married, sex will be an issue for you. That's why it's so vital to regularly evaluate your sex life.

What we've given is merely a launching pad. From this point, if you want your sex life to take off, then you need to sit down as a couple and talk about sex and intimacy in your marriage. Discuss what's good and what's not. Lovingly share concerns or hurts. Don't assume anything unless you assume that discovering sexual satisfaction will require adjustments from

Dr. Peter: The "Others"

As a counselor, I found this chapter especially difficult to write. For every chapter, we've had to weigh a wide variety of issues and themes, knowing that much will be left out. For the topic of sexual satisfaction, this was especially the case; however, there was an overwhelming sense that it would be a disservice to end the chapter without mentioning other information.

Many significant factors influence sexual satisfaction. This brief reference in no way diminishes their magnitude. (On the contrary, each of these issues is hefty enough to be it *own* book.)

Experiences and events that can affect sexuality in marriage are often traumatic or personal. These include sexual abuse, pornography, infidelity, stress, premarital promiscuity, impotence, and childbirth/having children.

Almost daily, I counsel with clients whose marriages are gripped by these issues and others. These couples face many unique challenges, often including dysfunction in sex and sexuality. If your marriage is similarly affected, you might need more help than what we've offered in this chapter. Professional counseling could be a necessary first step on your road to sexual satisfaction.

you as an individual. Remember that an extraordinary marriage requires sacrifice and selflessness. Don't change to get something for yourself (although that could be a nice perk eventually). Change because you value your spouse and because you value intimacy in your marriage—between the sheets and everywhere else.

Chapter 3 Follow-up
Discovering Sexual Satisfaction

Husbands, complete the sentence:

- When we got married, my expectations of sex were . . .

- In our marriage, the most exciting sexual experience was when _____ because . . .

- When it comes to sex, the easiest thing to talk about with my wife is _____ because . . .

- When it comes to sex, the most difficult thing to talk about with my wife is _____ because . . .

True/False for Husbands:

T/F   At times, I am uncomfortable discussing sex with my wife.

T/F   My wife understands my sexuality.

T/F   I understand my wife's sexuality.

T/F   In our marriage, sex can become leverage.

T/F   In our marriage, one spouse desires intimacy more often than the other.

T/F   In our marriage, I am sexually satisfied.

T/F   In our marriage, my wife is sexually satisfied.

Wives, complete the sentence:

- When we got married, my expectations of sex were . . .

- In our marriage, the most exciting sexual experience was when _____ because . . .

- When it comes to sex, the easiest thing to talk about with my husband is _____ because . . .

- When it comes to sex, the most difficult thing to talk about with my husband is _____ because . . .

True/False for Wives:

T/F   At times, I am uncomfortable discussing sex with my husband.

T/F   My husband understands my sexuality.

T/F   I understand my husband's sexuality.

T/F   In our marriage, sex can become leverage.

T/F   In our marriage, one spouse desires intimacy more often than the other.

T/F   In our marriage, I am sexually satisfied.

T/F   In our marriage, my husband is sexually satisfied.

Ask your spouse:

- What messages about sex (from your childhood, culture, church, etc.) have you carried into our marriage?

- What is one of your fantasies?

- What are some simple adjustments we could make to have a more satisfying sex life?

Discover sexual satisfaction this week:

- Block off time with your spouse for selfless intimacy.

THE CONCEPT

Developing a successful marriage is like riding a bicycle built for two. In order to go the distance, you have to spend a lot of time together, pedaling and steering in the same direction.

Sadly, many couples stop spending time together when they get married. Sometimes one hops off the bike completely, or they put something other than their spouse on the backseat.

Have you ever seen one person riding solo on a bicycle built for two? Wouldn't that look ridiculous? Does your marriage look ridiculous?

THE CONSTİTUENTS

We asked couples, "In your marriage, who benefits most from time together?" Responses:

The Husband: 4%
The Wife: 25%
Both: 72%

Spending Time Together

It's a wonder that anybody in America has time to spend together with a friend let alone a spouse. Between checking e-mails, Facebook, texts and twitters, answering cell phones, going to work, driving kids back and forth to sporting events, medical appointments, shopping for necessities, eating meals and the like, how does anyone get together! It's exhausting to simply think about it, let alone try and actually accomplish it. But if you want your marriage to grow or thrive to any extent, you have to spend time together. You have it make it a priority.

Years ago I (Dan) had the privilege of speaking for the Motor Racing Outreach ministry at professional racing events now and then. I got to spend time with the drivers, their crew members, and their families on race days and at other special occasions. I'm not gonna lie to you; it was pretty cool.

In my small role, I hung out in drivers' trailers and I smelled the fumes on Pit Road. I can tell you from experience that the cement floor in the garage area is so clean you could perform brain surgery on it. I watched drivers' families sit on edge with every single loop around the track. (Bumping fenders at 200 mph, wouldn't you?)

One day—one of those unique nail-biting mornings—I stood in the main garage, observing the scene. Mechanics bustled, tools clanged.

Million-dollar vehicles and multimillion-dollar product placements waited in the wings. A driver's wife was standing nearby, and we knew each other, so we struck up a brief conversation. During our chat, I inquired about her family's life and asked how she and her husband were doing.

She shared a few family statistics, then she paused for a moment. Looking out over the glitz and chrome of the garage, her famous face displayed a flash of vulnerability. It could've been the stress of the weekend, the mounting tension of race day, or the fact that I was the "family guy" on set that morning—I'm not sure which—but something caused deep emotion in her voice when she spoke next. "Dan," she said, "I wish my husband loved me as much as he loves that car."

There the woman stood, decked out, camera ready, and sad. Ironically, the credentials around her neck read, "VIP."

In her husband's defense, I know the guy loves his wife. I've witnessed it. In fact, their marriage is an example to lots of others on the racing circuit. Still, the man's car is his livelihood, and on the weekend of a big race, it becomes his whole life. Thursday, Friday, Saturday, and Sunday, almost all his time is spent with the car—inspecting it, listening to it, testing it. He does all he can do to make sure he's ready come Sunday morning. With a race and millions in prizes and advertising on the line, it's easy to understand how, for a few days each month, the career and the car could become so all-consuming. It's also easy to understand how, for a few days each month, the man's wife could feel tossed aside.

Time Problems

It's a cliché, but it's worth printing nonetheless: The best way to spell *love* is t–i–m–e. Time together is one of the most important, most necessary elements in a successful relationship. Still, of all the things a couple can let slide in their marriage, time together is one of the most common by far. It's not only NASCAR personalities who have trouble balancing the hours. From boroughs to farmlands, subdivisions to trailer parks, men and women everywhere in America find it difficult to work each other into their schedules. For a variety of reasons, their time together has earned only a low rung on the priority ladder.

Many husbands and wives find themselves in this category for one simple reason: They're suffering from incompatibility shock. When the honeymoon phase of their relationship wears off and they get wrapped up in day-to-day odd jobs and errands, they're surprised to realize they have very little in common. Suddenly the initial attraction that drew them together is no longer enough to compensate for their different personalities, backgrounds, interests, views, and preferences. He likes classic car shows and live rock bands; she prefers Broadway shows and classical music. She's a homebody; he would go out every night if he could. Her idea of a great Saturday is a fancy brunch and shopping with her girlfriends; he would rather spend the morning in perfect quiet, sitting in the woods, waiting for a deer to cross his path.

We can easily detect the makings for disparity and conflict within couples like these. When it comes to the way they each spend time individually, there is very little or nothing that draws them together. What one likes the other dislikes, and vice versa. As a result, it can be difficult and frustrating to spend time in each other's company because the two view the world completely differently.

Incompatibility shock isn't the only thing that hinders a couple's time though. Many husbands and wives, even the very compatible ones, struggle to be together for other reasons. Some, whether they share hobbies and interests or not, have a simple problem: They just don't get excited to be together anymore.

As is common in relationships, the greater the familiarity, the more energy it takes to discover something that feels new or interesting. The longer spouses are together, the more time and work are required to reach new depths of closeness, intimacy, and fun. So even if two people are bored with their current relationship, often they still don't want to devote the kind of effort needed to reach a better level. For many spouses, it's easier to pursue other friendships, activities, and hobbies, finding excitement in something brand-new instead.

In addition to this sort of laziness and to incompatibility shock, there's another common threat to a couple's time together, and this one is possibly the most widespread and dangerous of all.

A Common Pitfall

John and Marie were both in their late forties when their daughter moved out of the house to go to college. This left only their son at home with them, and he had just passed his driver's exam. Suddenly, John and Marie had one child living out of town and the other child driving all over town. To say the least, the couple's household pace slowed considerably.

As their two children were growing up, John and Marie had built great relationships with them. They had thrown birthday parties, gone to all the soccer games, and talked through teenage crises late into the night. Their kids loved them. Even so, as their children's independence increased, John and Marie found themselves facing a surprising dilemma. As many parents do, they had worked so hard at being good parents that a necessary part of their marriage relationship had fizzled in the process. Recognizing this, they were both surprised. "We're going to have to learn how to spend time together again," John admitted to friends.

> Their lives are crowded by life, and they're distracted from their relationship by a host of decent, commendable things.

Without realizing it, John and Marie had fallen into a common marital pitfall: They stopped fitting each other into their own individual schedules. He was busy trying to be a good dad; she was busy trying to be a good mom. Both had admirable priorities in mind, but in the process, they were blinded by one huge mistake: They lost sight of their marriage.

Between responsibilities at work, commitments at church, outings with friends, activities for the kids, hobbies, and everyday tasks, it's quite simple for spouses' days to become filled beyond overflowing. This is especially common among couples with young children and couples weathering crises (health, financial, or coping with aging parents). Their lives are crowded by life, and they're distracted from their relationship by a host of decent, commendable things. They become obligated to so many people, places, and programs that they can't squeeze out a spare moment for each other.

What's really bad about this one is that on the outside the people stuck in this pattern seem as if they're doing well. They make good money, they manage good relationships, they volunteer for good causes, and they raise good children. As a result, their kids adore them, their friends compliment their willingness to listen, the local schools and organizations can't get enough of their service, and they're very successful on the job. Yet their success hasn't come without cost.

These people have foolishly chosen to put their occupations, their playtime, their talents, even their church or their children first above all else. This happens at the expense of a marriage. Yes, even good things can be bad for a marriage. Often when spouses fill their calendars with too many relationships and duties—regardless of how important those relationships and duties are—they successfully allow their own time together to get bumped right off the agenda. What should be number one becomes number one hundred.

Whether it's because of compatibility issues, boredom, or distractions, couples may experience a lapse in their time together, but it's extremely unwise to let that lapse persist. If a couple wants to maintain a healthy relationship, they must put a high priority on the moments shared between the two of them. For a successful marriage, time together is absolutely necessary.

Growing or Drifting?

There's a strong correlation between the health of a marriage and the amount of time the two spouses spend together. The link between those two variables is astounding. At times, it seems possible to predict how healthy the marriage is based on the number of hours the husband and wife spend together. (We'll talk more about this in the next chapter.)

Couples who are thriving report they are striving to have a regular dating time or at least a regular dating life; they go out together at least two times a month. On the other hand, couples who are struggling usually report they seldom spend time together. They usually say they can't remember the last time they were out with each other. That's not a great report.

Couples who are thriving . . . are striving to go out together at least two times a month.

Husbands and wives clearly need one-on-one time together. It allows them to engage in real, adult, meaningful conversation. It gives them the chance to let loose and have fun with each other. It creates opportunities to connect and relate to each other. Without interactions like these, a relationship gets stale. In fact, among couples who haven't spent time together for a while, when the concept is reintroduced, the health of their relationship usually improves drastically.

More than merely a nice or a fun addition to a husband and wife's bond, time is an essential part of a great marriage. They can't merely take it or leave it. They can't wait and see if they'll have a free evening that will allow for a dinner date between the two. That's not enough. If they're not spending time growing closer, they're undoubtedly drifting apart.

Dr. Peter: The Latent Effect

Over the past few years, Shawn Maree and I have felt compelled to encourage our children to develop their own unique talents and abilities. For us as parents, it's been exciting to watch as the three of them gain confidence, skills, and self-esteem in pursuing different areas of interest. It has also been very busy.

Depending on which kids are involved in which activities, certain seasons of the year tend to be more hectic than others. Most seasons, we've managed our family schedule fairly well. Still, over the course of a few particularly frenzied months, we really let things get out of control.

One particular fall season, our son had football practice for two hours every weekday and football games most Saturdays. Both of our daughters had soccer practice once a week and soccer games every Saturday. Shawn Maree and I both had church commitments and social obligations. In addition to that, I was scheduled to travel a couple times on business.

For the first few days—even the first couple of weeks—of the fall, we did OK. Shawn Maree and I checked in with each other regularly, usually making plans for handing off our kids. That communication was all we had time for, but it was enough to keep life moving forward.

Looking back, it's obvious what happened between my wife and me that fall. At the time, though, it was slight and subtle. We simply began to drift. Unintentionally, we had let our relationship drop significantly down our priority list. As a result, we went from talking a lot (several times throughout the workday with longer chats in the evenings and on weekends) to seldom having any conversation that contained depth or meaning.

Although Shawn Maree and I were spending less and less time together, at first we didn't notice any problems. But over time, little cracks began to appear in our relationship. We traded negative comments. Our interactions were laced with confusing messages, then misinterpretations, then misunderstandings, and finally, full-blown arguments. Tempers were flaring and hurt was surfacing; what little time Shawn Maree and I had together was not enjoyable. We held on to frustration and found ourselves avoiding each other. As the family wheels were going 100 miles per hour, our marriage wheels were stuck in the mud.

Throughout this two- to three-month period, I, as the counselor, continually analyzed myself, my wife, and our marriage. *What's going on?* I wondered. *When did it start? Why am I so frustrated? How did it get so bad in such a short time?* We'd had a great summer. We'd known the fall would be busy. The kids were excelling. *Why is she so selfish? Won't she see that I'm trying my best to do it all?*

Then one day enough was enough. I had a near meltdown. Frustrated, I called my wife to schedule a meeting. A little while later, we met each other in a Barnes & Noble parking lot and went inside for coffee. There, we confessed feelings, shared thoughts, spit out accusations, and flared our tempers yet again. Still, I was determined to keep cool and get to the bottom of what was going on.

> When a husband and wife neglect to be together, eventually it takes a serious toll on their relationship.

As my wife and I continued to talk, we both laid down our pride and confessed the root of the problem: We hadn't been spending time with each other! Admittedly, that core issue had become muddled and had turned into all kinds of other things, but the basic glitch was rather uncomplicated. Shawn Maree and I were barely spending enough time together to maintain a casual acquaintance, let alone to sustain an intimate marriage. That day, we acknowledged several things: We still loved each other and we were still committed, but we needed to make a change.

What Shawn Maree and I found, as many other couples discover far too late, is this: When a husband and wife neglect to be together, eventually it takes a serious toll on their relationship. They might go on for weeks or even months before they experience any ill effects, but sooner or later evidence of the gulf between them begins to show. Normally, this doesn't happen gradually but all at once. Something—anything—will set them off, and the two will become negative with each other, bickering about trivialities and getting upset over insignificant issues. This phenomenon is something I call the latent effect.

After enduring a long period of marital distance, a marriage suffers greatly. The two spouses get frustrated and irritated with each other, and the relationship usually requires serious mop-up work. However, when they realize they're under the latent effect, they're often in a bad position to change things. They're so distant that the last thing they want to do is spend time together.

The more time two spouses have spent apart, the harder it will be for them to reconnect. However, there is also good news. Even if a couple has considerably abandoned each other—even if they're living basically separate lives under the same roof—a lack of time together is relatively easy to remedy.

Marriage Time Zones

Many couples almost never spend one-on-one time together. They either don't go out together at all, or they make a habit of always joining up with friends. This does not benefit a marriage.

The reason time together is necessary between spouses is that it is very closely linked with many other important aspects of a relationship. When a husband and wife make a habit of carving out special moments solely for each other, that commitment benefits a host of things: communication, friendship, emotional connection, and sexual intimacy, to name a few.

Time together opens channels for deeper bonds and better conversations. This allows for stronger emotional ties, which often lead to a deeper level of sexual intimacy. Focused time also lets two spouses set goals, make plans, and dream together for their future. Especially for spouses with children, it allows a space for them to rekindle their own relationship and to be reminded of why they got together in the first place. This could possibly explain why, in general, husbands and wives who hang out with each other end up liking each other even more.

If a husband and wife want to experience rewards like these, they should strive to spend time together on each of four different levels. This time doesn't necessarily have to be spent outside the house, but it does have to focus on growing the relationship:

1. *Connections:* Build a routine of spending one-on-one time together every day. Aim for at least twenty to thirty minutes daily, and use the time to touch base on what's going on in your lives. Share exciting news, family updates, stories from the day, and information about people and circumstances you encountered. Also take care to confer on administrative issues, such as work schedules, upcoming events, and minor challenges.[10]

2. *Dates:* Make an effort to go out together weekly or bimonthly. Set aside an evening, a morning, or an afternoon, and leave your work and children (if you have children) behind for a time. Take a walk, have dinner at a restaurant, catch a movie, go for a drive, or just sit on a park bench and people-watch together. Use these special times for one of two purposes:

    *   *Coasting*—Keep things light. Focus on enjoying each other's company. Hang out and spend time doing your favor-

10 If you have young children, this may often seem difficult, but it is vital for your marriage. In addition, as your children see you taking time together, they will begin to see how important your marriage is to the family dynamic.

ite activities. Smile, laugh, hold hands, and develop your friendship.

- *Working*—Intentionally deal with one or more issues/problems that have surfaced in the scope of the marriage. These could include anything from money to parenting to extended family issues. If a problem is developing, spend the necessary time to find a solution together.

3. **Extended Dates:** Once every month or two, go on longer dates (several hours) or a full day away, with little on your agenda aside from relationship building. This allows you a chance to let your guard down and have in-depth sharing. Go shopping in another town, take in a ball game, or go for a hike at a state park. Get outside your usual surroundings; this "away" factor allows for more openness and relaxed interaction. These dates can be as inexpensive or as lavish as you'd like, depending on where you go and what you do. (Especially because, if you have kids, there's no need to get an overnight babysitter.)

4. **Getaways:** Once or twice a year, schedule an overnight date or a weekend/weeklong escape. Make it an anniversary present or a seasonal retreat, but make sure to get away. Rent a hotel room, a cabin, or a beachfront bungalow. If finances don't allow for that expense, take the kids to Grandma's house and hole up at home—as long as it means you and your spouse can have extended time alone, together. If your workplace allows, you can even piggyback a getaway onto a conference in order to split some of the costs. However you arrange it, do it. See the sights, go out for a nice dinner, and spend the time connecting sexually. Most importantly, relax and give your relationship what it needs to rekindle and refresh.

> Spending time with your spouse will require compromise.

For many couples, a list like this is the license they need to get away with each other for a refresher course on their marriage. However, a fair number of other couples will look at this list, baffled. *How will we ever spend thirty minutes together without completely running out of things to do?* they'll wonder. They're not used to being left alone with each other. They're not accustomed to sharing their hours or their activities. Individually, they can fill their calendars, but they're at a loss when it comes to working as a pair. They have plenty of things to do in life, and plenty of things they like to do, but they have very little they like to do with each other. Not only is this sad and frustrating; it's also a sure sign that two people have gone far too long without spending time together.

Even two very different spouses can find common uses for their time. While both may not exactly *love* the activity, they can at least find something that both of them like. This is easily illustrated by discussing movie preferences. He loves action flicks and she loves documentaries, and both of them get some enjoyment out of romantic comedies. When they're looking for something to do together, a romantic comedy provides a good option. Although it wouldn't be a first pick for either one, it's still an excellent choice because it's something they can enjoy together.

Unless you've married a clone of yourself, spending time with your spouse will require compromise. In order to develop this area of your relationship, you may need to develop new skills or explore new interests. If your spouse loves doing something, give it a try. If you can develop an appreciation for your spouse's preferred pursuits, it will be much easier for the two of you to spend time together. Try your hand at rock climbing or learn to like museums. Learn the basics of football or take a shot at baking if that's something your husband or wife loves. Even if you never *really* pick it up yourself, you can at least love being with your spouse. After all, that's the ultimate goal here.

Spending time together in marriage is more than just hanging out when the two spouses happen to have spare time. Spending time together is reflective of a couple's commitment to each other. Although sometimes it's spontaneous and natural, most of the time (especially when two people aren't used to it), it's intentional, requiring dedication and planning. For many couples, it demands ruthless loyalty that, at times, might even seem to border on recklessness.

Meeting in the Middle

Imagine two spouses on a stage, separated by a variety of other people and objects. In the space between the husband and wife, there are a briefcase, a TV, a few in-laws, a couple of kids, a computer, exercise equipment, a bucket of cleaning supplies, and a few friends. These are samples of the things that come between a couple, keeping them from spending focused time together.

On a stage, these objects and people serve as a huge barrier. In life, the barrier is even more formidable. These days, men and women are continually beckoned by causes and concerns that can quickly fill the hours in a day. There's nearly always something on the stage between us.

When two people are divided by objects, the only way for them to meet in the middle is to sidestep the objects. Even better, they could toss the objects aside. In the same way, when spouses' time together is hindered by time at work, with the kids, at church, or watching ESPN, the only way to fix that problem is to sidestep a few other commitments and activities.

Are we suggesting you disregard important relationships and responsibilities? Are we saying you should quit your job, abandon your kids, and stop going to church? No. But we are suggesting that you do everything in your power to maintain time together. If this requires letting go of some other meaningful commitments, you should let go. If it requires making the kids feel left out occasionally, let the kids feel left out. If it requires forgoing other hobbies and responsibilities, bow out. Why? Because if there's one thing you as a couple should keep toward the very top of your priority list, it's time shared between the two of you.

You might have many commitments. Countless good causes could benefit from a chunk of your schedule. The rest of the family would always like more time with you. But you have only twenty-four hours in your day and only one partner in life. What good is it to neglect your spouse and instead fill your calendar with lesser commitments?

Chapter 4 Follow-up
Spending Time Together

His & Hers:

Of the list below, husbands, circle your favorite ten activities, and, wives, star your favorite ten activities:

Bike riding

Picnicking

Ice skating/Rollerblading

Walking on the beach

Stargazing

Watching fireworks

Taking a hot-air balloon ride

Going to the movies

Joining a coed sports league

Cooking a meal

Horseback riding

Parasailing

Camping

Remodeling

Gardening

Going for a drive

Playing laser tag

Bowling

_____

_____

_____

The activities that both of you pick are prime examples of ways you can spend time together. Put one on your calendar today!

Ask your spouse:

- What commitments/priorities/hobbies/relationships keep us from spending time with each other?

- What commitments/priorities/hobbies/relationships can we get rid of?

- Are we managing all four marriage time zones? (See pp. 67–68.)

- When we have couple time, how much of that time do we spend coasting and how much do we spend working?

- How soon can we schedule another getaway?

Spend time together this week:

- Take inventory of your schedules. Do they promote time together, or do they make it nearly impossible for the two of you to be alone with each other? If they promote time together, good job! Plan a date for your earliest overlapping time slot. If, however, your schedules get in the way of time together, do whatever it takes to change them. Remember, be ruthless.

THE CONCEPT

Your spouse is a wealth of delightful surprises, with the potential to be your closest friend. Trust us, there's more good stuff in him or her than you can even imagine. You might need to dig deep and take a good look around, but if you do, you'll be amazed at the treasure you find.

How long has it been since you've lifted the lid?

THE CONSTİTUENTS

We asked couples to complete the phrase, "In our marriage, friendship matters more to". . . Responses:

The Husband: 4%
The Wife: 11%
Both: 85%

Chapter 5

Developing Genuine Friendship

We debated throwing out this chapter completely. After all, isn't friendship what you would naturally expect to happen when two people spend enough time together? If a husband and wife can practice the things we outlined in the previous chapter, do they really need this one? Why follow with this topic? Why not merely move directly to the next topic?

The onset of social media in America has elevated friendship to an entirely new level. On sites like Facebook, people can rack up thousands of friends. Twitters that tweet can have followings that equal or surpass that number. With the availability of so many potential friends, could it or does it diminish the friendship between a husband and wife?

In observing couples, we can't help but notice a definite distinction between the time spouses spend together and the level of friendship they share. The two elements aren't necessarily related. In some marriages, couples spend hours and hours together and are still not close. In other marriages, couples spend little time together yet claim to be best friends. What's the deal?

The deal is that there are so many distractions competing for your time and attention, that friendship, the most basic element in a marriage, could easily be brushed aside like crumbs from the dining room table. Time together may not be the only measurement of the level of friendship a couple shares but we still agree that it's an important component.

Although we are keeping friendship separate from time together, we are piggybacking them in this book. Friendships must follow time together—kind of a package deal. In the end, what good is a friendship without time together and what is time together if you don't have friendship?

Together Yet Apart

It's possible, of course, to spend large quantities of time with another person without ever developing that relationship into a friendship. Many people in the workforce encounter this truth—despite shared lunch hours, group projects and tasks, and plenty of time to chitchat, coworkers often remain distant from each other. Even though their schedules overlap for countless hours on a daily basis, they never grow close. We can call them acquaintances but not exactly friends.

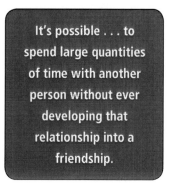

It's possible . . . to spend large quantities of time with another person without ever developing that relationship into a friendship.

In the same way, a husband and wife can share a life without sharing a friendship. They can spend all their mornings, afternoons, evenings, and nights together without ever watching their relationship move beyond a regular, unexceptional familiarity. Such is the case with one couple we'll call Shane and Rachel.

If there were an award for passing time with your spouse, Shane and Rachel would win it, hands down. The husband-and-wife duo is paired almost constantly—day trips, dinners out, afternoons with the grandkids, corporate events, and church picnics. They're there, and they're there together. In addition, Shane runs his own business, and Rachel helps out at the office, so they get to see each other during the workday too.

If time were all it takes to develop a genuine friendship, Shane and Rachel would be the epitome of married couples. You could chain them together at the waist, and it would barely affect their daily routines. Nonetheless, their relationship can't be described as a friendship because it's missing some of the key elements that are sandwiched between friends.

The Friendship Sandwich
effort, depth, support

Of all the ingredients that compose a friendship, we're going to specifically emphasize these three. If these ingredients are developing between a husband and wife, the two spouses have more than a marriage. They have something that ties them together, makes them an alliance, gives them a camaraderie that can't be matched. It's the friendship sandwich—great to chew on.

Ingredient 1: Effort

The first element of friendship is the most central and the most foundational. It's also the element most often overlooked. Of course, *effort* is easy to overlook in a number of new friendships. In the beginning stages of a friendship, often both people will be having so much fun together that the relationship work will feel effortless. It will seem natural for them to prioritize the relationship, to disclose their thoughts and feelings, and to fill their time with laughs, smiles, and cozy, friendly moments.

It's likely that at the beginning of your relationship with your spouse, you could identify with this sort of thing. Back then, what existed between the two of you was all fun, flirting, and heart flutters. Effort didn't apply to the relationship at all, unless you count the work you both put in when you were dressing for your dates.

> In the beginning stages of a friendship, often. . . the relationship work will feel effortless.

As your relationship progressed, though, the novelty wore off and difficulties crept in. You remembered you don't care much for his favorite pro wrestling hero; you decided her passion for knitting isn't enough to help you find any enjoyment in yarn. Or you discovered she's not cheerful in the morning; you found out he's got an unfortunate love for baked beans. Over time, some of the enjoyable, romantic elements of your relationship crumbled. Undoubtedly this helped you to realize that, on some days, effort is required for the two of you to get along.

> Friendship is a doing thing—you have to spend time together, and you have to make sure your time together is good.

The main difference between friends and people who merely spend time together is this: Friends enjoy their time together. This isn't an issue of quantity alone; this is about a quantity of quality. Friendship is a *doing* thing—you have to spend time together, and you have to make sure your time together is good. Don't expect a cozy relationship with your spouse if you're almost never having fun with each other. If you aren't making efforts to laugh, giggle, share jokes, and experience exciting activities as a couple, it's highly unlikely that the two of you are friends.

Sneaking Away

A few years ago, my (Dan's) wife put forth effort that taught me a great lesson about developing friendship in marriage. Jane had known for a long time how much I love golf. There was really no way for her to avoid knowing it; I had bugged her almost weekly to go play a few holes with me.

On several of these occasions, she caved and spent an afternoon on the golf course with me. Still, those experiences weren't much fun for her. She hadn't had any training in the game, and I had played for years. Our skill levels were so mismatched that, when we played together, Jane felt she was hindering me.

So one day, unknown to me, my wife signed up for golf lessons. For a while, I went on with life as usual as Jane was secretly sneaking away so she could learn how to play the game. She studied grips, practiced keeping her head down during her swing, and came to understand the difference between a driver and a five iron.

In time, Jane improved at golf, to the point she actually began to like the game. She had a great time when I asked her to go out on the course, with me, and she even began to suggest days when *I* might want to go with *her*. It was fantastic.

I asked Jane once what made her want to learn how to play golf. Her response was simple. She said that since I enjoyed the game so much, she wanted to enjoy it too. That way, when the two of us wanted to go out and do something fun together, we could both have a good time golfing.

Have I mentioned that my wife is great?

Ingredient 2: Depth

Ask someone to list his or her friends, and you could get a wide range of responses. No doubt you'll hear about social networking friends, golfing buddies, shopping companions, work colleagues, and neighborhood pals. There will be friends who get together once a year, friends who meet for lunch every Wednesday, friends who call each other a couple times a week, and friends who spend time together every single day. You'll hear about relationships that have been in the works for a few months, a few years, and a few decades.

> He wants to be fully known by her. She wants to be fully known by him.

With so many friendships out there, it's easy to see they're not all on the same level. Some are powerfully deep; others are still working to move beyond superficial. That's because there are tiers of intimacy in relationships—as two people disclose more of their inner selves to each other, they experience more depth as a couple. The more they get to know each other, the closer they become.

In essence, friendship is about knowing and being known. This is a common desire in all human beings, which is why people can get such delight out of a good friendship. Individuals have an innate longing to be understood and appreciated by others, to experience life with a community around them. We want people to know us.

This fact is certainly not lost in marriage. Husbands and wives want to be more than merely familiar with each other; they want to have a meaningful exchange of knowledge between them. This isn't

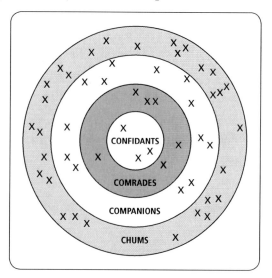

only about the facts either. It's about discovering the intricacies in someone, about having a profound awareness of another person. He wants to be *fully* known by her. She wants to be *fully* known by him. But how do they get to that point?

We propose that, in general, there are four different tiers of friendship. These can apply to any of your relationships, but we'd like you to think of them in terms of your marriage. We'd also like you to think of them in terms of a target:

Imagine that every person everywhere has a friendship target and that each of his or her friendships is a specific spot on that target. Every relationship hits the mark in one of the following categories:

- *Chums* are friends whose interests overlap yours in one specific area. You both like the same music or go to the same church. You have memberships at the same gym or investments in the same company. Your kids are the same age, or your offices are in the same building. This overlap creates opportunities for you to be in the same place at the same time. You have conversations because they're convenient, and you get to know surface details about each other: name, age, education, job, and so forth. Still, although you enjoy each other's company, you could hardly say that you really know each other.

- *Companions* are friends who spend time with you on a semiregular basis. Instead of merely bumping into each other, you make time for each other. You're committed to the friendship, so you plan activities to do together. When you talk, your conversations aren't limited to merely the facts of your lives. Your relationship is strong enough that you can share your opinions on important issues, and you're not afraid to disagree. Still, you don't disclose everything to each other; although you've moved beyond the surface, the friendship is still shallow.

- *Comrades* are friends who want to talk to you even when you're having an off day. Your relationship is enjoyable, but it's not limited to fun only. Typically, you've walked through meaningful circumstances together. Comrades have seen the good and the bad in you, and they still like you anyway. You enjoy being with them, and you can be comfortable with yourself when they're around. You trust them enough to share your concerns and fears, your beliefs and pursuits, your problems and pains. You ask them for advice, and when it's given, you often take it.

- *Confidants* are friends who know you to the core. More than only details or specifics, they know you. Confidants know your dreams and your history, your successes and your disappointments, your sources of joy and your sources of grief, your strongest strengths and your most embarrassing weaknesses. If you were a language, they'd be fluent. You trust them to the point that you can feel comfortable telling them anything. Nothing is off-limits. These are the people you seek out when you need some-

  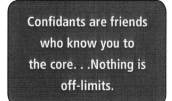
  Confidants are friends who know you to the core. . .Nothing is off-limits.

  one to celebrate or cry with. Their opinions matter to you—when you're trying to make an important decision, you want them to weigh in. Confidants have spent enough time with you to recognize your emotions and pinpoint your behavior patterns. More than that, though, they understand why you react and behave the way you do. They'll coddle when you need coddling, but they're also willing to give you a swift kick in the pants, so to speak. Put simply, confidants *get* you and understand that you need them. The closeness of your relationship is proof.

The thing about these different tiers of friendship is that they each take up a different amount of space. Like the outer rings on a target, the friendship tiers that take less energy are the easiest to hit. There's more room reserved for them too. It's possible to have a thousand chums, but we have energy for a much smaller number of comrades. It would be foolish to try to be incredibly close with all our friends. No one has that much time or energy to give.

Without distinct boundaries in our friendship tiers, we would spread ourselves too thin, and every relationship would suffer. We have to be choosy with people, maintaining a nice variety of chums, a good bunch of companions, a select group of comrades, and a limited number of confidants. As we move toward the center of the target, there are fewer people in the circle, but there is more depth.

The Marriage Target

Spouses should ask themselves:

- How deep is our marriage?
- Have we ever been deeper or shallower?
- How much of ourselves do we share with each other?
- What don't we understand about each other?
- Is there a topic that's off-limits in our relationship?
- Have we kept secrets from each other?
- Do we keep conversation on the surface, or have we dug further than that?
- Does one spouse dig more than the other?

In marriage, the ideal level of friendship is a bull's-eye every time. That's what you're shooting for after all—to know best and to be known best, to achieve the deepest levels of disclosure with each other, and to build a relationship that is extraordinary by any comparison. You might have a few people in that center circle, but your spouse should most certainly be one of them. Is she? Is he?

There's a little more to it than just that though. Your spouse should be in the inmost circle, but he or she should also be *the* center of your relationships. It's not good enough to give your husband or wife a spot that's merely near the top; your spouse should *be* the top.

Outranked

It was an ordinary day for Elaine but only because she was completely out of the loop. Elaine's husband, Malcolm, and his best friend, Kevin, had met for some male bonding, which they did on a regular basis. Nothing about this particular outing seemed unusual to Elaine until, after having been gone for a couple hours, Malcolm returned home with the title to a brand-new boat. It had a price tag of fifty thousand dollars and was identical to the boat Kevin had bought that day,

Elaine was surprised to see a miniyacht parked in her driveway. Why wouldn't she have been? Her husband hadn't mentioned the purchase to her at all. Malcolm hadn't initiated a call, a conversation, or a single attempt at marital communication before he signed on the dotted line. From his perspective, this splurge was strictly a buddy thing. Elaine's input wasn't a concern or even a factor in the decision.

A marriage didn't dominate this husband-and-wife relationship; a friendship did. The his-and-his floating playgrounds made that perfectly clear. In choosing to buy a boat with his friend without consulting his wife, Malcolm had effectively ranked the two relationships and it's pretty clear which ranked higher.

Of course, this affected Elaine's opinion of her marriage. How could it not? Her husband had disregarded her completely, dismissing her thoughts, opinions, and right to have a voice in the matter. From the status of their finances (now significantly in debt) to the details of the boat itself and the addition of a hitch on one of their vehicles, Malcolm had made all major and minor decisions as Kevin's friend, not as Elaine's husband. When it came to communication, he had been open with the friendship and closed with the marriage. In order to have a fun new toy, he had ignored his wife, overlooked her, and cast her aside. In the future, how could she feel important to him?

Selective Circling

Often, people choose to be less open with their spouse than they are with others. Instead of having a spouse who is also a best friend, these people have a spouse *and* a best friend. When something significant happens in life, they call the best friend first, not the spouse. When they're in trouble, they look to the friend, not the spouse. When they need advice, they want the friend's opinion, not the spouse's.

This is a big problem because instead of promoting unity between a husband and wife, it promotes disunity. Jealousy and doubts can easily creep in, and, let's face it, marriage is difficult enough without stuff like that.

To be more open with your spouse than you are with anyone else, there's one thing you must do: Be more open with your spouse than you are with anyone else. It's as simple as it sounds.

If you want to be selective about your best friendship, all you need is self-discipline. Learn to hold back information from others if you haven't yet told your spouse. If your spouse has something to share with you, listen. If your spouse calls you on the phone, do your best to always pick up. Reserve certain topics for your marriage relationship alone—this will enhance the level of friendship in your marriage. Make your marital conversations and disclosures a major priority.

Ingredient 3: Support

We've talked about how friendships need effort and depth; now let's tackle the third ingredient: support. "No man is an island."[11] It's not healthy for individuals to exist in a vacuum, void of relationships to sustain them. Friendships have a way of bracing us as people. They make us better. They make us stronger. They help us to hold up under difficult circumstances.

---

11 John Donne, "Meditation XVII," from *Devotions upon Emergent Occasions, 1624.*

Dr. Peter: Lopsided Communication

During counseling, rarely does a wife admit that her husband tells her too much. More often I hear a wife complain that her husband doesn't tell her nearly enough. She feels she's communicating either more deeply or more regularly than he is, and she's disappointed that she doesn't see more interaction on his part.

This observation is not surprising because women are generally more verbal than men. Still, it should be taken very seriously. Lopsided communication can make a marriage quite dissatisfying for the spouse who's carrying the heavier load.

In discussing support within a marriage, we could talk about several different topics. We'd like to keep this simple, though, so we're going to focus on only the most significant. Like many of the other things in this book, the concept is something so basic it could seem almost unnecessary to mention. Yet, from observing our own and others' marriages, we know that this is an ingredient we can't *not* bring up. Are you ready for this?

Be there.

Be there.

BE THERE!

If you want to have friendship in your marriage, you need to support your spouse. If you want to support your spouse, you need to be there. And where is "there"? It's where your spouse is. Being there means showing up for the marriage, geographically and otherwise. It means putting in an appearance, standing alongside, taking a hand, offering a shoulder, cheering from the most sensational of experiences to the dullest of everyday moments. It means being there for your spouse, not for yourself. And how do you know when you're being

> It's very possible that the most powerful gift we can give to our spouse is the gift of two good ears.

there for someone other than yourself? That's easy. When you're being there for someone else, most of your time is spent listening. Yes, we really mean that—mouth shut, ears open, *listening*.

The most treasured friends have one key thing in common: They take the time to really hear you. More than merely being quiet, more than sitting there, more than tuning out, they're engaged, they're interested, and they're working to understand. A good listener is invaluable. When you find one, you don't easily let go.

It's very possible that the most powerful gift we can give to our spouse is the gift of two good ears. Husbands and wives who listen well cultivate marriages in which trust comes readily, disclosure happens often, patience is displayed fully, understanding is reached quickly, and friendship blooms wholly. Yet listening well takes respect, genuine concern, and selflessness, which means listening well doesn't come naturally to most of us.

If you have a tendency to space out, butt in, offer easy answers, speed up the chatter, forget key points, doze off, change the subject, or keep one ear tuned elsewhere, then we have a group you can join. Let's all say it together:

"Hello, my name is *[your name here]*, and I stink at listening."

"Hi, *[your name here]*. Welcome to the program. Now that you've acknowledged your problem, you can begin to take steps to move beyond it."

We considered coming up with twelve steps, just to be cute, but we decided that would be overkill. Try six steps instead:

1. ***Send the right signals.*** Let your body language convey your interest and concern. Maintain eye contact, lean forward, nod,

avoid fidgeting. Set aside other projects so you can offer your full attention as a listener.

2. *Ask questions* that will help you understand the circumstances.

3. *Tolerate pauses and silence.* People are more likely to open up when you allow for time in which they can do so.

4. *Prepare for follow-up.* Treat the conversation as if it's something to be remembered. Pay attention to details so you can ask about them again later.

5. *Listen.* Keep your mouth shut and let the other person steer the conversation. Often people care far less about hearing solutions than they do about seeing real concern.

6. *Let it be awful sometimes.* When another person is hurting, often the shallowest reaction in the world is "It'll be OK." Easy answers like that dismiss pain. When something is awful, acknowledge it as such. *Really acknowledge it* before you try to move ahead.

By developing active listening skills—by being there—you help to supply one of your spouse's inherent needs. You create a place in which she can open up and connect. You help him to be truly known. Listening builds bridges between people, and they're absolutely necessary. After all, no man or woman should be an island. We need each other.

Come to think of it, our need for support is so big that we need more than only each other.

Friendships and Trampolines

The same way no individual should exist in a vacuum, no marriage should exist in a vacuum either. As a man or a woman needs support, a marriage needs support as well. Although your spouse provides you with some support, you can't expect him or her to take care of everything.

Like the fabric on a trampoline, people seek to be supported from a number of different angles. From family concerns and job issues to religious beliefs or a desire for laughs, we all have countless areas to attach a good spring. Friendships are those springs.

In a healthy marriage, a spouse will be supportive in a number of different areas. He'll have a knack for helping you get through struggles at work, or she'll figure out how to help you handle your extended family. He'll share your passion for some things, and she'll have great insight on some of your biggest concerns. Still, in some areas your spouse's supportive contributions won't fit the bill. In those areas especially, you need other people.

When a trampoline is missing a few springs, it throws off the bounce completely. When springs get rusty, the bounce gets snappy. In the same way, when a person fails to fill key friendship needs, his direction begins to waver. And when he lets friendships turn stale, things get harsh. The condition of the relationships determines the condition of the individual.

> When pursued to a healthy degree, additional friendships . . . greatly enhance the stability of a marriage.

A wife needs the support of other women and wives because there are certain things her husband can't even hope to comprehend about her life. A husband needs the support of other husbands and men because there are certain things his wife won't even begin to understand about his life. When pursued to a healthy degree, additional friendships like these greatly enhance the stability of a marriage. They affirm and enhance us as spouses, helping us to become stronger individuals. Then when we come together again, the marriage is stronger too.

Are there people in your life who encourage you to develop and grow individually? Do you have friends who support you as a husband? As a wife? Beyond that, do you have supportive friendships with other marriages? Can you think of a husband and wife who are helping you get better and who have your best interests in mind? Are there couples who show you how to avoid the common surprises and pitfalls of married life? Are there people whom you're supporting in the same way?

If not, it's time for you to start. After all, springs shouldn't be neglected. Without the support of the springs, the fabric can't function as it was intended.

Friendship is a necessity for healthy living—for you, for your marriage, and for others around you. It requires effort, depth, and support. When those three ingredients are present, friendship is delightful, like a big, crazy bounce for your marriage. Try it; you'll feel you can fly.

Chapter 5 Follow-up
Developing Genuine Friendship

His & Hers:

Multiple Choice: Select the response that best fits, then take time to discuss your answers.

1. How would you characterize your friendship with your spouse?
   a. We're chums.
   b. We're companions.
   c. We're comrades.
   d. We're confidants.

2. Which aspect of friendship is most developed in your marriage?
   a. Effort
   b. Depth
   c. Support

3. Which aspect is least developed in your marriage?
   a. Effort
   b. Depth
   c. Support

Ask your spouse:

- On a scale of 1 to 10, with 10 being the best, how well do I listen to you?

- In what ways can I improve my listening skills?

- Which other friendships are the springs that support us, individually or as a couple? Are there friendships that hinder our relationship more than help?

- Are we at the center of each other's friendship circle? How do we know? If not, how can we change that?

- How has our friendship changed over time?

Develop genuine friendship this week:

- In at least one conversation with your spouse, apply active listening: Send the right signals, ask questions, tolerate pauses, prepare for follow-up, let the other person steer, and let it be awful sometimes. Watch how this simple practice affects your communication and your marital friendship.

THE CONCEPT

Like it or not, physical attraction plays a role in marriage. Often it's one of the initial things that draws two people together. And on the flip side, when a relationship is going downhill, physical attraction is often one of the first things to go.

We must take care of our bodies and appearances.

This doesn't mean all women should look like supermodels.

This doesn't mean all men should have biceps bulging out of their sleeves.

But looking your best goes a long way in helping your spouse be attracted to you. You'd be crazy to ignore that.

And, of course, there's much more to it.

THE CONSTİTUENTS

We asked couples to complete the phrase, "In our marriage, attractiveness means more to . . ." Responses:

The Husband: 15%
The Wife: 14%
Both: 71%

Chapter 6

Valuing Physical Attraction

Americans are obsessed with image. Not just personal image, but the image projected by the home they live in, the car they drive, the clothes they wear. There is no question that appearance is an often distorted, overhyped issue, but we're not going to avoid it simply because there's the potential that the discussion might get off track or offend people. In exploring physical appearance/attraction, many variables carry significance. We will not mention them all, but we'll take a stab at it to get you and your spouse talking because whether we like it or not, beauty is a very big deal—big enough, presumably, to hold two people together.

It seems that looking good has become one of life's ultimate accomplishments. On TV and the Internet, advertisers constantly communicate that (for women especially) outer appearance matters more than anything else. Even our economy rewards a certain standard of beauty—the skinniest models and the most attractive athletes can get the biggest paychecks and the best endorsement deals, sometimes regardless of talent or skill.

Beauty worship extends far beyond the media too. Our societies worship at the altar of youthfulness, promoting clear skin, toned muscles, and full lips at any cost. As a result, men and women alike starve themselves and attack their bodies with scalpels in order to conform to a specific set of acceptable physical attributes: narrow noses, wide eyes, smooth foreheads, large breasts, and washboard abs. In the United States alone, the American Society of Plastic Surgeons reports that more than 10 million cosmetic procedures are performed each year. The business grows every new day. It seems beauty comes at a price and Americans are more than willing to pay.

Our culture is saturated with false images and out of touch with reality when it comes to beauty. Still, despite our distorted concept of beauty, it is foolish to suggest that physical appearance doesn't matter at all. Merely because it's unhealthy to be fixated on a desire for beauty, that doesn't mean *any* effort toward allure is inherently unhealthy. After all, a natural part of being human is the desire to be found attractive.

Take, for example, the high-school reunion. Or the thirtieth birthday. The day of your wedding. The day of someone else's wedding. The Big 4–0. Six months after childbirth. Six years after childbirth. The corporate Christmas party. The job interview. The Big 5–0. Family picture day. These are significant milestones in life, and they're also days when most of us want to look good. Why? Because being attractive matters to us. The way we feel about the way we look is part of what defines us. It also contributes greatly to the status of our relationships.

In marriage, physical attraction plays an important role. For most couples, physical attraction was the spark that first drew one spouse toward the other. "His eyes were twinkling all night!" she squealed to her roommate. "Her legs looked good in that skirt," he bragged to his friends.

Physical attraction can generate a powerful magnetism between two people, especially in the beginning of a relationship. What we often fail to recognize, though, is that appearances continue to be a driving force throughout the duration of a marriage. In particular, there's one marital area in which physical attraction plays a part. It's significant, but most of us don't pay it much attention. As a matter of fact, when it comes to this area, we often don't notice it until we're already far gone.

Fair Expectations

Previously, we introduced the concept of CHDs (constant happy discoveries), noting that most marriages begin in that phase. There, everything seems rosy and wonderful, and you can't imagine thinking your spouse could be anything but the ideal marriage partner. Alas, as it has been said, all good things must come to an end.

Most marriage relationships eventually move beyond the era of CHDs and begin to plateau at lower expectations. Over time, as a husband and wife get to know each other better, their surprising, jubilant revelations about each other happen less often. There's nothing wrong with this; it's natural, healthy, and expected. However, it also brings a new vulnerability into the relationship. When a couple's protective "We're always happy" bubble pops, they face new risks. Relational hazards they had been shielded from before become very real dangers. Specifically, instead of bounding around in marital glee, couples can find themselves caught in the downward spiral of *perpetual negative discoveries*. That's right, you've met the CHDs; now meet the opposite PNDs.

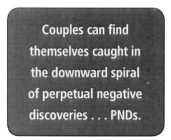

Couples can find themselves caught in the downward spiral of perpetual negative discoveries . . . PNDs.

Take note, we did call this an extreme. It's perfectly healthy to discover that some things about your marriage (and even some things about your spouse) are less than ideal. To a degree, negative discoveries in relationships come with the territory. After all, no two people are going to be thrilled with *everything* about each other all the time. And yet, there is a line that can be crossed—when suddenly you're finding more than only a few slight annoyances in your marriage or in your spouse. Suddenly, it's beyond dirty socks on the floor and an irritating chewing habit. Somehow, something snowballs, and your negative thoughts about your spouse and your marriage begin to roll downhill, picking up speed and volume along the way. This happens when the *P* gets tagged on to your NDs, and then things get dangerous.

Here's what all this has to do with looking good: When it comes to perpetual negativity in marriage, matters of appearance can often be the trigger point. As physical attraction often serves as the spark in uniting two people, a decline in physical attraction often marks the beginnings of division. Admittedly, this statement might connect more with husbands than it does with wives, and for good reason.

Intuition and Oblivion

As men ourselves, we'll be two of the first people to acknowledge that men are not nearly as intuitive as women. Women have a keenly developed awareness about all things relational; they detect even the slightest changes in people and situations around them. Then they make all these little connections in their heads and figure out what's *really* going on. It's fascinating how talented they are. On the flip side, if you want a man to detect that something is amiss, you pretty much have to hit him over the head with it.

I (Peter) am especially amazed at this in my own marriage. My wife graduated college with a business degree, while I've always studied the social sciences. Given that fact, you would think that I should be more advanced in reading our relationship than she is, right? But I'm not. Compared to her, I'm oblivious at recognizing negative changes that happen between us. If an aspect of our marriage fades, Shawn Maree notices it long before I do. Judged against her sharply tuned insight, my internal barometer has dropped to the bottom.

This is a common gender difference in marriages. Most of the time, men are simply not as aware of relational nuances as women are. When it comes to perception and insight, wives are setting major-league records while husbands struggle to make it in the minors. That's why, for husbands especially, appearance plays such a key role in the marriage.

As hard as he might try, a man will probably never be able to interpret relational shifts as well as a woman can. A wife might experience two really low weeks before her husband will begin to fathom the possibility that something is wrong. Her girlfriends will catch on of course; the inflection in her voice will clue them in immediately. But in order for him to notice, something more obvious is required—specifically, something more visual.

To be blunt, we husbands probably won't make the connection that your recent quietness means you're still upset about yesterday's argument. We might not catch on when you're having an exceptionally bad day. It's likely that we won't think anything's out of the ordinary, even after a thousand hints, conversations, and nonverbal cues. We're not wired to understand that kind of thing. But if you develop dark circles under your eyes, if your hairdo starts looking overgrown, or if your clothes don't fit as they used to, then we'll get concerned. We'll play back the events of the past few days, and we'll rack our brain in an attempt to figure out what went wrong.

This might sound shallow and pathetic, but it's true. It often takes a change of the wife's appearance to make a husband sit up and take notice. This is not because he cares more about how his wife looks than how she feels. Really, it's not. Mostly it's because, on the whole, men can't read feelings or behavior the same way we can read looks. We're good at the visual stuff, but when it comes to moods, circumstances, and subtleties, those things aren't on our radar.

Of course, this is a delicate issue, and some husbands don't even come close to treating it as such. When it comes to a woman's looks, too many men are insensitive, uncomplimentary, and completely tactless. They don't understand how important it is to admire their wife. They can't fathom the fine balance between honesty and criticism. They haven't yet figured out that there's no good answer to "Do these pants make my thighs look huge?"

It's clear from the start these men haven't learned the cardinal rule of body image in marriage: When it comes to matters of physical appearance, both husbands and wives should always be careful to maintain sensitivity.

Creating Magnetism

In matters of attraction, couples can tend to get lost in the details or hung up on measurements. She's bothered when his outfit isn't exactly event-appropriate or stylish; he's continually negative about the way she cuts her hair. She gets frustrated when she gains five pounds; he gets upset when his hair begins to thin. Their concept of physical attraction is all about expectations, and it's no good for the spouse or for the marriage. What *is* good for both the spouse and the marriage is for couples to look at each other with two objectives: to be attractive and to be attracted. The distinction here is subtle yet very dramatic.

If being attractive to your spouse can pull you together even an ounce more, isn't that worth the effort?

If there's any person in the world you should desire to attract, it's your spouse. With no exceptions, your husband or wife should be the primary audience you seek to please when it comes to the way you look. Rather than working to look good for your friends, neighbors, coworkers, family, or the public in general, your spouse should be the first spectator you have in mind when you try to look good.

Marriage is difficult to begin with. Why not make it easier on yourself and your spouse? If being attractive to your spouse can pull you together even an ounce more, isn't that worth the effort? If you can enhance your marriage by capitalizing on your charms that your spouse finds attractive, why wouldn't you?

Physical attraction is one of the things far too many couples fail to take advantage of. Instead, they put very little effort into being found attractive within their marriage. They stop working out, they gain unhealthy amounts of weight, or they wear unflattering clothing. In general, they stop caring. Yet these same people, after a divorce, will often behave quite differently.

At the end of his first marriage, Alex was an out-of-shape, overweight, middle-aged man. But almost as soon as the divorce was final, Alex suddenly was motivated about the way he looked. He signed up for a gym membership and got on the fitness track. With uncharacteristic vigor, he hit the weights and did the cardio, and in a matter of weeks, Alex was fit and trim. And dating.

Alex had caught the eye of a new woman, Marsha. Within a few months, he proposed to her and they tied the knot. Settled into his new relationship, Alex gave up his workout routine. His muscles shriveled back to flab, his stomach grew back to jiggly, and he went back to looking like someone who didn't care very much. At the end of his second marriage, though, he started caring again. With a second divorce under his belt, Alex renewed his gym membership.

We're not about to say that Alex's whole life revolved around the size of his waistline. As with any relationship, there's no doubt that much more than looks played into the beginnings and the endings of Alex's two marriages. Even so, the man's habits are indicative of something that happens in many marriages today. As soon as they land a mate, they stop fishing for compliments and let themselves go. Then, if that first marriage doesn't work out, they undergo a total body makeover when it's time to play the dating game again.

They sign up for yoga class, buy a new wardrobe, get a charming haircut, and spend hours under lights at makeup counters in the mall. Why? Because they want someone new to find them attractive; they know physical attraction is the spark in a new relationship. This makes us wonder: What if those same efforts had been made toward

A Change of Perspective

Lynn is a bright-eyed, well-dressed woman in her early fifties. Kind, dignified, and elegant, she is also overweight. She wasn't always this way; the pounds seem to add up along with the years. Now her weight has turned everyday tasks into difficult obstacles. Running errands and walking up a slight hill require extra effort because of her extra weight.

For Lynn's husband, James, it's another story. Strong and trim, he's in excellent shape for a man of any age, and he's close to sixty. His vigor and healthy body put many younger men to shame.

Some people, in observing James and Lynn together, have commented that the husband is fit and his wife is quite out of shape. By today's cultural standard of beauty, of course, this longtime, happily married couple doesn't seem like a compatible match. In fact, even one of James's close friends once asked him how he had managed to stay attracted to his full-figured wife. it was the kind of brutally honest question that can be shared only between friends, and James's response was just as matter-of-fact.

"Well," he said, "I struggled with it for a while, but then I looked at her one day, and I simply decided that she was the standard. I told myself that no other woman was as attractive as Lynn. I wouldn't let myself believe anything different." James stopped, then continued with a smile. "And now, when I look at her, she is so beautiful to me."

maintaining the original spark? Would the flame of that first marriage still burn brightly?

Like everything else in life that's important, a major factor of physical attraction is commitment. It takes commitment to stay attractive *for* your spouse. That's the first part of this picture. The second part focuses on something even more important: It takes commitment to stay attracted *to* your spouse.

Let's face it, appearances change and youthfulness fades, maybe not on TV or in magazines, but it does in real life. Wrinkles, flab, and drooping are bound to happen. After pregnancy or surgery, a human body isn't the same. Over time, muscles shrivel, hair becomes sparse, posture wilts, and earlobes keep getting bigger. It's unrealistic and unfair to expect a person to forever look twenty-three. It's also unrealistic and unfair to assume that attraction between spouses happens spontaneously.

Just as it takes work to remain faithful to a spouse, to spend time with a spouse, and to cherish a spouse, it also takes work to remain attracted to a spouse. It's a choice you make, plain and simple. Just as James did, you can choose to make your spouse the standard. Instead of letting your gaze wander to the faces and forms of others, you can choose to feast your eyes on the person you married. Here are suggestions:

- Pay attention to your favorite part of your spouse's appearance. Compliment it on a regular basis.
- When in conversation with your friends, speak highly of your spouse's looks.
- When you've got time to daydream, picture your spouse—in the way you find most appealing.
- Whistle when your spouse walks by.
- Keep a framed picture of your spouse on prominent display where you work.
- Practice gazing at your spouse. When you look at him or her, plan on being delighted.

Now, for a word on everybody else: With 6 billion people in the world, you're bound to find a few of them attractive. This is a risk only if you allow it to become one. Sure, often you can't avoid experiencing an initial attraction to someone other than your spouse. But you *can* stop it from going beyond there.

If you find yourself attracted to someone other than your own husband or wife, there are steps you can take to stop:

- Limit your contact with the person. If you don't have a compelling reason to interact with that person, stay away.
- Be boring. That's right, tone down your charming self! Keep your conversations and behavior from being special or exciting. Use only basic politeness.
- Avoid comparisons to your husband or wife. The other person hasn't earned the right to be considered within the same realm.
- Speak highly of your spouse in the other's presence. Even casual references to your marriage can serve as boundary markers; they remind you of your devotion while also communicating that devotion to others.

A big part of attraction is training your brain to look away from others and toward your spouse. As you practice this, your spouse becomes your standard for attractiveness, and your attraction to your spouse becomes a knee-jerk reaction. When this happens, you're in for something spectacular.

Trials and Years Together

Mac and Carol have been married for more than thirty-five years, and their relationship is surprisingly optimistic, under the circumstances. In fact, one of the first things people notice about Mac and Carol is that their outlook on life is positive. The two have a certain depth to them, as if they've been rooted in a special concoction that nobody else knows about.

Carol has sincerity that's like a warm day and grace like a cool breeze. She loves to send people gifts out of the blue. Mac's whole face flashes when he smiles, and he gives the impression that he has all the time in the world for anybody. He also likes to pull pranks on his grandkids regularly. On the surface, everything appears to be rosy. Yet neither Mac nor Carol has traveled a smooth path, and the path ahead will be bumpy.

Carol lives with rheumatoid arthritis, a disease that makes tasks such as washing dishes nearly an entire morning's project. Her hands curl up as if they're clasping lemons, and her joints are in almost constant pain. Mac has multiple sclerosis, which impairs his vision, speech, balance, and coordination. He uses an electric lift for the single flight of stairs in his home, and sometimes a cane isn't enough help when he wants to walk.

Still, Mac and Carol have acquired the key to understanding beauty. It's so evident that when others spend time with them, they barely notice Mac and Carol's physical battles.

A few years ago, Mac and Carol went to dinner at the home of friends. The couples sat around a table to chat. During their conversation, it was noted that Mac and Carol had undergone trials in their years together. Mac elaborated about their ordeals. He spoke particularly about how Carol braved her arthritis.

Carol, true to form, cut in by shaking her head and saying, "Well, we're not as strong as we used to be, and these hands are old now."

Without missing a beat, Mac reached for Carol's hands and took them into his own. He looked down at them and then began to talk about how much he loved her. Running his fingers over her arthritic ones, he said, "I know what these hands have done. I've watched what these hands have been through. I've seen them keep a home and wash clothes and care for children." As he softly traced some of the darkened spots on Carol's hands, Mac went on matter-of-factly.

"I love these hands," he said, "more today than I did when I put this wedding ring on her finger because I've seen all the things that she has done for me over the years."

The room was silent when Mac finished speaking. His words lingered, as if no one around wanted to disturb the beauty in the air.

That is a marriage.

There was a time when Mac's legs were strong enough to carry him up a flight of stairs and back again without any trouble at all. There was a time when Carol's hands were capable of opening envelopes and popping pickle jar tops. Back then, neither person had smile wrinkles or crow's feet. According to modern beauty standards and cultural expectations, both spouses were more attractive then.

However, beauty is in the eye of the beholder. When love deepens between two people, they become more attractive to each other over time. Beauty becomes less about facial symmetry and a waistline measurement; it instead encompasses the whole person. Love changes our perception so we can see the whole person—exterior and interior alike. When flabby rolls appear, the backside begins to sag, a bald spot shows up, muscles get soft, or skin crinkles up like used tissue paper, we can still be pie-in-the-sky attracted to each other.

The best of us have developed an attraction based on the entire person. That way, we can value attraction even when abs turn into flabs. After all, any rookie can get all fired up when somebody young and lithe walks into the room, but without skill, he'll fly the coop at the first sign of a droop. It takes the talent of a veteran to *stay* committed, despite love handles.

Chapter 6 Follow-up
Valuing Physical Attraction

His & Hers:

On a scale of 1 to 10, how much does my physical appearance matter to me?

> He says: 1 2 3 4 5 6 7 8 9 10

> She says: 1 2 3 4 5 6 7 8 9 10

On a scale of 1 to 10, how much does my spouse's physical appearance matter to me?

> He says: 1 2 3 4 5 6 7 8 9 10

> She says: 1 2 3 4 5 6 7 8 9 10

How important to you are the following?

> Very (V)   Somewhat (S)   Not at all (N):

He says:	**She says:**	
_____	_____	My spouse maintains an active lifestyle.
_____	_____	My spouse maintains a balanced diet.
_____	_____	My spouse maintains a healthy weight.
_____	_____	My spouse experiments with new looks.
_____	_____	My spouse's appearance is neat.
_____	_____	My spouse smells good.
_____	_____	My spouse is clean (clothing, breath, etc.).
_____	_____	My spouse compliments my appearance.

Ask your spouse:

His or her opinion about you:

- What attracted you most when you saw me for the first time?

- What is your favorite thing about my physical appearance?

- Which of my outfits is your favorite?

- How much does society influence your thoughts about appearance?

His or her opinion about himself or herself:

- What do you like best about your own physical appearance?

- What do you like least about your physical appearance?

Opinions on health:

- Do you think I have a healthy lifestyle? Why or why not?

- In what ways could I promote a healthier lifestyle in our home?

Value physical attraction this week:

- Spend a little time primping first, if you'd like, then grab a camera, grab your spouse by the hand, and go outside to take some pictures. Find a park or a cool old building, and spend time snapping shots of each other there. Have fun with it: make funny faces and bedroom eyes for your photographer spouse. Or hold the camera at arm's length and get some good kissing pictures of both of you. Then pick your favorite photos and frame his-and-hers prints to display at home, at the office, in the car, or on the bedside table.

THE CONCEPT

Emotional connectedness is a blending of two mind-sets. It's very difficult, like making a smoothie from a whole apple and a whole orange.

Chasing emotional connectedness requires a sacrificial, selfless, surrendering type of lifestyle. This doesn't come naturally to most people. Still, the more you practice it in your marriage, the smoother your blend will be.

And the smoother the blend, the sweeter the marriage.

Come on, take a drink.

THE CONSTİTUENTS

We asked couples, "In your marriage, who needs to be more emotionally connected?" Responses:

The Husband: 5%
The Wife: 22%
Both: 73%

Chasing Emotional Connectedness

We've already established that couples in America are struggling to find time to spend together and develop genuine friendship, so doesn't it make sense that chasing emotional connectedness is even farther from their reach?

People rarely speak face to face these days. Who hasn't witnessed a husband and wife sitting in the same room either texting each other or sending instant messages on their computers? We snicker and shake our head, but the truth is, in America, we are slipping farther and farther away from finding emotional connectedness. The elusive emotion that we continue to chase is almost a thing of the past, of days gone by, something that occurred in other generations before the advent of technology.

And yet, we've probably all witnessed it—those couples you've seen shuffling down the sidewalk. Gray-haired and hunched over, they lean on each other's forearms and talk with wrinkled smiles close to each other's ears. Aside from their matching polyester pants and his-and-hers orthopedic shoes, the two share a visible connectedness, a link so tangible you can practically feel it when they walk by.

When the two of them talk, they finish each other's sentences. When they go out, they want to go together. When one of them is happy, the other feels giddy. When one is sad, the gloom cuts to the heart of the other.

They think the same. They react the same. They even *look* the same. Their relationship has a distinct, time-honored connection that comes from decades of shared love. Over time, their hearts have been woven together, deeply and profoundly, to the point that the most difficult of their wedding vows actually seems to have come true. The two have become one.

Yet there's something about those still-in-love older couples that makes the rest of us hope to have what they have. Maybe it's the softness in their eyes or the sparkle in their dentured smiles. Maybe it's the peace they've created that forms a bubble around them, defying age, pain, and circumstance. Whatever it is—even if you can't identify it—there's *something* between them. The bond is so powerful, it's like a magnet that draws you in. Even when you can't relate to it in the slightest, you're easily convinced it's something worth chasing.

We call this emotional connectedness, even though we're still not exactly sure whether that's what it should be called. It's emotional, yes, but not in a blubbering, sob-into-the-Kleenex-box way. There's something more mental, more durable, and more willful to it than the typical Hallmark movie special. And it's definitely about connectedness, but there should be a better word than that. There's a fondness in this, a sense of true understanding and shared thinking. It's connection but also much more.

What we're talking about is complicated and practically undefinable, but we're going to take a shot at it anyway. Why? Because this element is a crucial step in the building a marriage that stays together for life. It has incredible power to mold a couple together. It makes longevity seem like less work and makes love seem more instinctive. It can put a husband

and wife on the same page in a way that might surprise both of them. It can help keep attraction going strong, take sexuality to a whole new level, and bring arguments to quick resolution. Shall we go on?

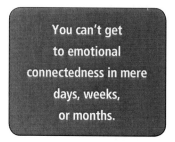

You can't get to emotional connectedness in mere days, weeks, or months.

OK, but what does it mean to connect emotionally? Or, more importantly, what does it take?

The bad news here is that you can't get to emotional connectedness in mere days, weeks, or months. Wanting it won't get you there. It takes years of hard work, a lot of love, and very hefty doses of "I'm sorry" to reach this level. The good news, however, is very good. In only a matter of days, weeks, or months, you can begin to experience intermittent slices of the emotional connectedness you're looking for. As those slices add up, you'll be on your way, and you'll know it. You'll feel it with certainty, and it will be good. Then one day, you'll reach a stage at which *intermittent* is exchanged for *constant*. Little connections will string together, and you'll find you have connectedness. By that point, you won't want to imagine that your marriage could work in any other way.

Two Sets of Emotions

First, let's talk about emotions. In simple terms, emotions represent the way people feel about things. The term *emotion* is used to describe a wide range of sentiments and conditions, from the fear that comes when you're watching a scary movie to the lifelong love a parent has for a child. You can like something or you can despise it—they're both emotions, but they're displayed with very different intensities and in very different directions.

The range of feelings is so large and wide that, for the sake of clarity, we've divided them into two categories. The first set of feelings comprises short-term emotions, often referred to as *moods*. The second set makes up our long-term emotions, which we often call *values*.

1. *Moods* characterize our feelings on a moment-to-moment basis. These are often linked to events and circumstances in our lives or to people and things we encounter. Moods can be greatly affected by many things, including general health, hormone and stress levels, and recent amount of sleep. "I'm excited" is an expression of mood. "I'm happy," "I'm anxious," "I'm in the mood," and "You're moody" are other examples.

Dancing without Seeing Stars

Imagine that you grew up dancing the waltz. As a child, you gladly learned the steps, positions, and elegance of this dance. After years of practice, you had it down cold. You could waltz in your sleep.

Now imagine that your spouse grew up dancing the jitterbug. He or she learned completely different steps to completely different music, wearing completely different costumes to boot. Like you, your spouse became quite adept at dancing. Like you, your spouse was accustomed to a single dance.

So when your waltz takes their jitterbug hand, there is a massive collision on the dance floor. Although both choreographies are beautiful in their own right and are executed impressively, they are far from compatible.

This is precisely what happens when two different value sets get married. Both can bring only themselves, and they can't help it that they don't instantly identify with each other. The husband brings his values to the floor and the wife brings hers, and the music stops. The tempo is no longer in sync. Still, if they're committed to each other as partners, in time they will create a new dance, a collaboration unique to them. Relying on the best contributions from both spouses, this new dance pattern will complement their new, shared life.

Outsiders will recognize its beauty and comment that it strangely resembles a waltz. Or is that a jitterbug?

2. *Values* exemplify, not surprisingly, the feelings for what we esteem. These are the essentials that matter, that touch us on a deep level. Every person has his or her own unique set of values shaped over time and influenced by gender, ethnicity, education, family background, religious beliefs, and significant experiences. These values can range from the complex, such as relationships and religion, to simpler principles, such as whether to recycle or adjusting to another's routine.

If married couples are going to pursue emotional connectedness, it's important to consider both sets of emotions. Both are significant because both play a role in the ways each connects with others.

Moods and Broods

In the short term, certain moods are more likely and certain moods less likely to create bonds between two individuals. In general, when people are happy, excited, kind, and having fun, others find them enjoyable. And when two people find each other to be mutually enjoyable, a bond forms between them, sometimes immediately. Something as simple as a pleasant mood can work wonders in a marriage.

Does this mean that sadness, boredom, and anything less than circus-level excitement should be completely off-limits for you and your spouse? Of course not. However, take note and be careful to reserve a hefty dose of pleasant moods for your home life. If you're good-humored all day at work but can't be cheery at home, something is dreadfully wrong. Even when you're dealing with the heaviest issues at home, if there's one place where an agreeable attitude is a good idea, it's under your own roof.

At the same time, though, if there's one person you should be free to let loose with, it should be your spouse. A great marriage is one that makes it safe for the husband or wife to have an unpleasant mood every once in a while. This, however, requires wisdom on both sides. When somebody's mood plummets, work to make sure it doesn't completely take over.

If you're upset, overtired, or brooding over something, be careful to keep from hurting your spouse in the process. Guard your tone. Hold your tongue. Don't let it go on forever. And if your spouse is the one who's brooding, do your best to offer support without taking offense. Give him a chance to start feeling better. Give space. Give grace.

With moods, a little self-control and consideration go a long way. Husbands and wives who leave emotional latitude for each other will find their relationship benefits greatly as a result. But that's the first set of emotions; there's another whole set to consider. And with the other group, things tend to be more complicated.

Scooting toward the Middle

As we said, values are what really matter to a person, and each individual has his or her own set of them. Values are extremely complicated; sometimes they're as dependable as the sunrise, and sometimes they can surprise like a lightning bolt. People can value a state of being, such as stability or security. They can value a role, like being the decision-making friend or serving as the family peacemaker. They can value ethics, politics, goals and achievements, religious tenets, and reputations.

To make things more knotty, in times of crisis people often begin to value things they've previously been indifferent to. The absent son becomes involved in the family when his mom gets sick. The irresponsible woman becomes trustworthy when she discovers she's pregnant. The spender becomes thrifty when the debts come due. In a snap, relationships, responsibility, and resources become values. When push comes to shove, they matter.

Because values are so important and so complex, connecting in that realm provides one of the most intense bonds a husband and wife can experience. Even so, the bonding doesn't come easily.

When two people get married and seek to become one, they're still *two people*. Even though they pool their cash and live in the same place, neither one automatically loses his or her own individuality. In marriage, husbands and wives enter into a whole new world of problems they can unravel from separate ends, circumstances they can react to differently, conflicts they can resolve in opposite ways, and value sets they can completely disagree on. In fact, typically a husband's and wife's different cares and concerns take center stage when displayed together under one roof.

What happens is simple. For every value held by one spouse, the other spouse can respond in one of three ways. He can treat it as a value, too, which is nice for everybody. On the other hand, she can treat it differently, either as a *nonvalue* or as an *unvalue*. The distinction here is slight but significant. A *nonvalue* is the middle-of-the-road approach. You can remember it by N–O–N, for **not** **n**ecessarily valuable. People are indifferent about nonvalues; they couldn't care less, one way or the other. In contrast, people care about *unvalues,* but they care in a negative direction. People don't merely *not like* unvalues; people *dislike* them.

If routine is a value for somebody, he prefers things to stay the same. If routine is a nonvalue, she could take it or leave it. If routine is an unvalue, he prefers the opposite of routine. Given the choice, he'll take an erratic schedule any day.

In every marriage, there is a unique combination of values, unvalues, and nonvalues. In order for these to connect, the husband and wife have to do adapting and accepting. On both sides of the marriage, the spouses must make efforts to scoot toward the middle. They must learn to sacrifice their own individuality for the good of the relationship, and we mean this in the very best sense possible. Neither one gives up his or her own set of values, but both of them learn to give up what matters so they can eventually have what matters a lot.

Here is what matters a lot: something that affects one spouse deeply matters a lot.

What Matters Most

There was a point in Winning At Home's history when our finances were stretched. It was nothing too worrisome, but it was enough to make me (Dan) a bit nervous about the situation. On a regular basis, I went home after a day's work and ended up talking with Jane about the company's financial standing. I often suggested ways that our family could cut back on groceries, outings, and other expenses just in case.

I thought I was being a good, responsible husband, but Jane's reaction seemed cold. Whenever I brought up the subject, she shut down completely. She'd get quiet and reserved, leaving me to my own concerns, with the added frustration that my wife didn't seem to care.

One day, I snapped. After yet another conversation in which I shared my anxieties and she did nothing, I couldn't take it anymore. I stopped in the middle of the conversation and practically demanded to know why.

"You know, babe," I said, "it really bothers me that you don't seem to care about any of this stuff. I'm worried about what might happen to the company, and you don't even want to hear about it!"

It was quiet for a second. When Jane spoke, her response was not at all what I had expected.

"I'm sorry, honey," she said, "but when you talk about this kind of stuff, it takes me right back to when I was little, and I just . . ."At that, her eyes got wide, and she took in a big breath, the kind that's almost too much to handle all at once. Her voice choked.

In that instant, the stakes changed.

When my wife was growing up, her family was incredibly poor. Her parents were divorced, and she lived with her five siblings at their mom's house. Because she was responsible by nature, Jane carried a huge burden for her family. She started working at an early age to help buy groceries and take care of her siblings. Every day, every year was the same. There were mouths to feed, and there was barely enough food to go around As a teenager, Jane bought all her own clothes, bought herself a cheap, beat-up car, and eventually made it through college with substantial assistance from government loans.

When we got married, we didn't have much in the beginning, but we were living large contrasted to all that Jane had known before. We improved at saving, and soon our financial worries became minor by comparison. Still, as the years wore on, the topic of money could bring up vivid memories of Jane's past. When we were in the process of founding Winning At Home, Jane had only one question for our board of directors. What did she want to know? Whether or not we would have enough money to afford health insurance for our family. I thought she was joking at first, but she was very serious.

Because her childhood was spent in poverty, finances have the power to affect my wife in a might way. So when I was talking about potential financial difficulties, I didn't fully realize how intensely that could affect my wife. To me, financial difficulties were on par with a few bad rounds of golf. To her, financial difficulties were beyond overwhelming.

Nearly fifteen years into our marriage, I was beginning to realize how deeply my wife was affected by the issue of money. Unknown to me, my small list of financial concerns was creating an enormous catalog of concerns, bad memories, and fears for my wife.

The point here is simple. When I was continually talking to my wife about the company bankbooks, I wasn't doing anything wrong. I was expressing a value in my life—the value I place on solving problems by always talking. Still, by giving up my own preference and sacrificing a minor value, I could make a step toward appreciating a major value in my wife's life. In doing so, I could help us to gain a slice of emotional connectedness.

When I looked beyond myself and tried to see things from Jane's perspective, I could better understand why financial stability is such a value for her. I felt, on a smaller scale, what she felt. In the end, we were worlds closer than before.

In this particular case, my worries mattered. My wife's, on the other hand, mattered a lot. What was best for our marriage was what mattered a lot.

A Smoothie Analogy

The problem with two different value systems is that they can conflict continually. Even if both sets are completely noble, there's always the likelihood that one will end up trampling the other. He values the camaraderie and closeness they get from spending time at home as a couple; she values the encouragement and accountability that come in spending time with friends. She thinks a savings account is vital; he wavers on the issue. He thinks firmness is the best part to parenting; she says that's ridiculous.

Chasing emotional connectedness in your marriage is a lot like making a smoothie out of two whole fruits. Think of it like this: if you wanted to drink a combination of an apple and an orange, you wouldn't toss the two whole fruits into a blender and press the "start" button. No, you'd take the time to core the apple and remove its skin first. You'd peel the orange and throw out its seeds. And if you had any experience with a blender, you'd pull apart the orange into sections and cut the apples into chunks. That way, you wouldn't burn up a perfectly good motor for the sake of one smoothie.

Start by figuring out which values are essential and which will do nothing but clog up the mix.

In the same way, if you want to blend with your spouse on an emotional level, it's important to start by figuring out which values are essential and which will do nothing but clog up the mix. In every marriage, certain elements add to the flavor and texture of the relationship, while others simply subtract from the quality of the combination. Each spouse brings a little bit of both to the table.

Each husband and each wife has values that are helpful on the road to marital bliss. These are the fruit of the fruit—the parts that nourish the relationship and enhance its flavor. At the same time, every husband and every wife also holds on to some values that can be harmful to their marriage overall. Sometimes, they're harmful because they're not good. Sometimes they're harmful because they're good but they infringe on a value that's better. Sometimes they're harmful because they're not worth wasting time on.

Whatever the reason, the harmful parts are best left outside the blender. This is where the real work of emotional connectedness comes in—shedding the skin, throwing away the seeds, and chucking the core, so that, after a time, the best of both fruits can come together to form the freshest and most satisfying blend.

Being There

Several simple behaviors will help you pursue emotional connectedness. Here are a few:

Help Me Help You

Develop a relationship of vulnerability in which you can freely talk about moods and values with your spouse. Don't wait for him to ask for an explanation about why you've been negative lately; open up and tell him what's on your mind.

Ask Second-Tier Questions[12]

Pursue greater emotional depth in conversation with your wife. Instead of sticking to only the facts ("How was your afternoon?" and "Are you upset?"), ask questions that will get below the surface. Rather than learning *about* your spouse, begin to really learn your spouse. For example, if she tells you she's had a "tough week," second-tier questions would dig deeper:

- What about this week made it so tough?
- How long have you felt this way?

12 If this sounds like active listening (see chap. 5), that's no mistake. Not only does active listening help to develop a friendship between spouses; it also enhances their emotional connectedness.

- Are there things about our relationship that made this week tough?
- What does "tough" mean to you?

Pay Attention

Notice the things that affect your spouse. What does he react strongly to? What bothers him? What makes him chuckle? What makes him erupt with laughter? Tuning in to his behavior is a great way to better understand his feelings and concerns.

Mean It

Ask her how she's doing, and really care about her response enough to shut your mouth and listen to it. Listen, listen, listen—without offering advice or a solution unless she specifically asks for it. Let your posture, facial expressions, and tone of voice convey your true concern.

When you shed your own shoes in order to walk in your spouse's for a while, you can't help but experience new levels of emotional connectedness. You become closer, more intimate, more in sync. It's great. Still, that's not to say it's easy. In reality, some of the strongest marital bonds come under the worst of circumstances.

Connecting in Crisis

The summer after our third child was born, my (Peter's) wife Shawn Maree went back to work part time. At that point in the life of our family, we had a kindergartner, a preschooler, and a newborn at home. With packed schedules at work and three kids to care for and chase at home, my wife and I had plenty of reasons to be tired.

Considering that Shawn Maree had just given birth and had the added stress of transitioning back into the workplace, it seemed to make sense that she needed time to adjust. After a few months, though, it seemed the adjustment wasn't happening as quickly as we'd expected. Shawn Maree was worn out and overwhelmed. She managed to keep up with her schedule, but she got sick a lot.

Then one weekend in January, our family went out of town with relatives, and Shawn Maree had miserable headaches and flulike symptoms for the duration of the trip. On our first day back home, she still had a fever, so we decided she should get checked out at the local hospital, to be safe.

We went to the emergency room, and almost from the moment my wife's name was called, things were different. I'd been to the ER in the past for a few bad cuts and a friend's dislocated shoulder, but this visit was surrounded by an intensity I hadn't experienced before. Nurses and doctors fluttered in and out of the room, always carrying a hushed anxiety along with their tests and charts. After a while, the on-call doctor came in and gave us his best guess at a prognosis. He told us Shawn Maree had either an extreme case of pneumonia or it was cancer.

The next day, we were in another emergency room, and Shawn Maree was having surgery to remove the fluid taking over her chest cavity. We had been told that a biopsy would determine chances of survival. Hodgkin's disease would give us an 80-percent chance, but with non-Hodgkin's that statistic dropped to 20 percent. Waiting for the results was the scariest thing ever.

When we left that hospital less than forty-eight hours later, we knew that it was stage 4, 80-percent chance. To think, a week before our biggest concerns were flulike symptoms and headaches. Shawn Maree was immediately admitted to another hospital so she could begin chemotherapy treatments. After a couple days of that, she was released to come home—back to "normal" for a while.

In only a matter of days, everything had changed for our family. Cancer became a dark cloud over the house—over each of us individually and all of us together. Suddenly, we were faced with new fears. Scary terms and procedures became familiar. Time was marked by hospital visits. In the middle of our buzzing family routine, real life had been interrupted. For me personally, there was emotional whiplash.

Every day, after having counseled with a full block of clients, I would go home to three small children who needed attention and corralling, as well as a wife who needed a sounding board as she worked through her physical and emotional crisis of cancer. In truth, some days I didn't want to deal with any of it. After all, I was already in the middle of my own crisis. Worry and responsibility overwhelmed me. In the face of a life-threatening disease and an uncertain future, I was trying to juggle work, home, hospital visits, children, and many of the responsibilities Shawn Maree usually handled. It was exhausting, and I felt completely in over my head. I didn't know how I, myself, would survive the ordeal, much less be able to support my wife in the process. In all the turmoil, I craved moments of normalcy and quiet.

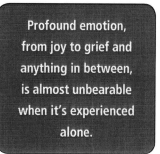

Profound emotion, from joy to grief and anything in between, is almost unbearable when it's experienced alone.

Many days, when I got home, I didn't want to ask Shawn Maree about her day. I didn't want to hear how awful it had been. I didn't want to face the inevitable questions about our future. I didn't want to watch her cry. I didn't want to think about her pain, and I didn't want to think about her needs first. I had my own needs, and they were pressing—I wanted to think about them, if I thought about anything at all. Most nights, I just wanted to sit on the couch by myself, put my feet up, scan a few columns from the latest sports magazine, and forget about all the junk I was trying to wade through.

Mountains and Valleys

Part of what makes all of us human is our desire to have people who will climb the mountains and endure the valleys with us. Part of what else that makes us human is our desire to crawl into a hole when a deep valley comes along. When tragedy strikes a marriage, it's easy for the husband or wife to become wrapped up in his or her own individual concerns and pains. In the process, they often unintentionally leave the spouse high and dry.

When you're entrenched in your own fears and doubts, often the last thing you want to do is help someone else—even someone you adore—as he wades through his fears. But in a marriage, when one spouse is hurting, it's important for the other spouse to be at her side. Profound emotion, from joy to grief and anything in between, is almost unbearable when it's experienced alone.

When your spouse is ecstatic about his new promotion, your shared excitement means the world to him. If she's anxious about the future, you can alleviate a few raw nerves just by talking with her about it. If he's upset about family ties, your sensitivity at the reunion speaks volumes. Sometimes, simply noticing the intensity of your spouse's emotion is enough because it means you're working to value what she values. It means you're *there,* which is exactly where you'd want her to be if the situation were reversed. It's exactly where you promised to be, "for better or worse, in sickness and in health."

We're not talking about a walk in the park. Take note; it's no mistake that we titled this chapter "*Chasing* Emotional Connectedness." As the story of your marriage plays out, emotional connectedness is a constant, unending pursuit. People change, situations change, stakes change. What brought you together in the beginning won't keep you together forever. The things that bonded you last year will be replaced by a whole new series this year.

Even when you find connectedness, you never really find it. That's the horrible, fascinating beauty. It's two becoming one—or at least doing their best to work in that direction. It's a lifetime of challenges and possibilities—the glory of the chase.

Chapter 7 Follow-up
Chasing Emotional Connectedness

His & Hers:

Individually, label each of the following as a

    Value (V): "I strongly agree."

    Nonvalue (N): "I could take it or leave it."

    Unvalue (U): "I strongly disagree."

He says:	She says:	
_____	_____	Families should eat meals together regularly.
_____	_____	Parents should finance their child(ren)'s education.
_____	_____	People should own vehicles rather than lease them.
_____	_____	When a couple has children, only one spouse should work outside the home.
_____	_____	A couple's in-laws should be allowed to visit whenever they want to.
_____	_____	If people want a good pet, they should get a cat.
_____	_____	Couples should regularly put a percentage of their income into a savings account.
_____	_____	In an argument, people should never yell at each other.
_____	_____	Families should set aside one day/evening each week for family time.
_____	_____	People should regularly give money to charities.

_____   _____   With credit cards, people should pay only the minimum requirement each month.

_____   _____   A couple's holiday plans should not hinder their parents' holiday traditions.

_____   _____   When watching sports, people should loudly voice their disapproval of athletes and officials.

_____   _____   People should attend church regularly.

Take time to discuss your responses:

- What are the primary value conflicts in our marriage?

- How do our value conflicts affect our marriage?

- In the areas where we disagree, what factors shaped our different values?

- What's one thing we can change to keep our value conflicts from limiting our emotional connectedness?

Ask your spouse:

- What does it mean for us to be emotionally connected?

- Am I getting the best of your emotional connectivity? Why or why not?

Chase emotional connectedness this week:

- Practice asking second-tier questions and paying attention. Rather than learning *about* your spouse, begin to really learn your spouse.

THE CONCEPT

At the front door: Many of us spend a lot of time making the outside of our home beautiful, creating curb appeal. We plant flowers, paint the shutters, mow the lawn, and clean the gutters. When people drive by, they see something immaculate and beautiful. From the look of things, the whole place is in harmony.

But at the back door: Far too many of us don't spend nearly as much time creating a home that's harmonious on the inside. A peaceful, content home is a piece of heaven. The alternative is a piece of hell.

What good is a pristine exterior when, on the other side of the door, relationships are crumbling, flaking, rotting, and dying?

THE CONSTİTUENTS

We asked couples, "In your marriage, who needs a peaceful home more?" Responses:

The Husband: 0%
The Wife: 1%
Both: 99%

Chapter 8

Guarding Home Harmony

According to the Family Violence Prevention Fund, one in every three women worldwide is a victim of sexual, physical, emotional, and other abuse during their lifetime. That adds up to about 1 billion abused women around the world every single year. According to an organization known as ChildHelp, a report of child abuse is made every 10 seconds. The National Center on Elder Abuse estimates that a million seniors are abused in some way every single year.

It doesn't take long to figure out that families in America are not living in harmony with one another. What appears to be picture-perfect and beautiful on the outside of a home, does not extend past the front door. Once inside, the image is blurry, as people are out-of-focus with one another. People are spending far too much time hitting one another and not hitting the high notes or singing as one.

Some of this occurs because people bring different backgrounds to the forefront. He grew up in a home where fighting occurred often, never escalated to the point of abuse, but issues were worked out with a high-level of emotion. People expressed anger through elevated voices and stinging barbs. She grew up in a home where more dust could be found than conflict. People kept their feelings to themselves and the only time voices were raised were when grandma came to visit.

People don't always realize how their different backgrounds and the way they were raised will affect their ability to live together and achieve harmony in their home. But we believe in can be done starting with awareness and ending in compromise and understanding.

I (Peter) grew up in a home in which conflict was resolved through yelling. My family's arguments were real blowouts; we'd scream at each other from beginning to end, and when the conflicting parties had all finally squawked their piece, the conflict was over and the people moved on. In contrast, Shawn Maree grew up in a household in which everyone was calm and polite all the time. People never raised their voices, even when they were upset with each other. Needless to say, combining those two different styles had the potential for a volatile eruption in our marriage.

Almost immediately following our honeymoon, Shawn Maree and I had the chance to spend a week in Puerto Rico, where she was traveling on business. Although we weren't together much because of her meetings and appointments, it was still good to be there with her. After all, we had been married only a week, and we knew that on returning home to Indianapolis life would quickly become real again.

We had no idea. During our first few days back in town, we realized our car needed new tires. There was a local mechanic, two miles away from our apartment, so we decided to take it there. Since I wasn't yet working and didn't need to drive anywhere, we agreed that I should drop off the car. Our plan was that I would deliver the car to the mechanic around noon, then Shawn Maree would meet me at a fast-food restaurant just around the corner from the shop. That way, my loving wife and I could share a bite to eat on her lunch hour, and she could drive me home so I wouldn't have to walk.

As planned, I dropped off the car and walked to the restaurant. I checked my watch; it was a few minutes before noon. I took a seat and politely waited for my new bride to pull into the parking lot and bounce toward me, dripping with wedded bliss. I waited and I waited. Moments dragged on, but Shawn Maree was nowhere in sight.

After ten minutes of waiting, I was confused and concerned. After twenty minutes, I was disappointed and annoyed. Since this was the age before cell phones, I had no way to contact my wife and see what was going on. To make matters worse, I hadn't taken any cash with me, so I couldn't eat. At 12:45, seeing no other option, I made my way down the busy five-lane road that led to our place and trekked home; there weren't any sidewalks. With every step, anger and hurt swelled inside me.

Not only was it fiery hot on that June day; the sweltering walk home gave me plenty of time to heat up emotionally. On reaching our little apartment, I was fuming. Sweat rolled down my face, and at a frenzied speed my brain questioned Shawn Maree's loyalty, integrity, and honesty. *Does she really love me? What is she really all about? What kind of woman have I married? Did I make a mistake?*

I slammed the door, kicked off my shoes, and stomped around for a while, preparing to give my new bride both a phone call and a piece of my mind. Just then, Shawn Maree entered the apartment, looking harried and frustrated. The air between us was instantly tense; it was as if an argument had started before either of us said a word.

Since she was obviously wrong, I expected instant groveling. Instead, she came at me with an accusation.

"Where were you?" she asked me.

Those three words were all it took. They were barely off her lips when the wrath of God (or something close to it) came spewing out of me. With my voice raised and my muscles clenched, I unleashed all the pressure and conflict I had felt in the preceding two hours.

As my decibel level intensified, Shawn Maree's face transformed before my eyes. Her expression changed from concern and confusion to disbelief and devastation. She explained later that our "conversation" was completely unfamiliar territory for her. She had never had anyone come unglued like that. While she was growing up, if her father ever made even a snide comment, it hurt her feelings. So being cut apart with words by the "man of her dreams" she was going to spend the rest of her life with was horrifying.

From my perspective that day, my behavior was not only legitimate, it was exactly what I was used to. In the heat of the moment, I could tell that my new bride was alarmed at my response to her, but that didn't make me stop. I had grown up with the understanding that bellowing was necessary to solve conflict. When I had a valid frustration with someone (and sometimes even when it wasn't valid), I let him or her know—in no uncertain terms—how I felt. Before I could let go and move on, I certainly took time (and decibels) to vent my concerns.

Communication and Conflict

Most divorces in the United States occur in the second year of marriage. Why do people divorce or separate so early on? Many counselors feel it's because of the inability of recently married couples to communicate effectively and resolve their differences. Hurts and misunderstandings are inevitable in any new marriage. Many people who separate and divorce are those who can't forgive, reconcile, and restore closeness after these times of conflict.

Studies show that couples who received training in how to communicate and resolve conflicts better showed a huge increase in marital satisfaction, communication, conflict resolution, and forgiveness.

The key is in the training. If you're in the first couple of years of your marriage or even beyond, and you want to have a satisfying and lasting marriage, read books, watch videos, go to retreats, and get counseling, all in an effort to improve and sustain your marriage.

So I kept yelling, for several minutes, until Shawn Maree had to leave and go back to work. She was crying as she walked out the door, but I didn't feel badly about it. No wife of mine was going to treat me like a piece of trash, especially only two weeks after our wedding.

After she left, I sat alone in our apartment and tried to calm down. I grabbed some food, turned on the TV, and stared at both blankly, still steaming inside. It wasn't until then that I noticed the blinking clock on the VCR.

My stomach churned as I looked from the clock to my watch and back again. There was an hour's difference. I bolted off the couch and craned my neck to see the clock in the kitchen. Surely it wasn't true!

It was. After returning to Indiana from trips to Michigan and the Caribbean, I hadn't remembered to turn my watch ahead an hour. I had berated my new wife and had sent her back to work in a wash of tears, all on Puerto Rico time.

Difference Is Necessary

Let's get one thing straight from the beginning: Home harmony is a beautiful thing, but often it's much easier said than done. In fact, possibly the most difficult part of marriage is learning how to cram two very different people into the same household. As one man said, "All marriages are happy. It's the living together afterward that causes all the trouble."

> Unless there are two separate entities existing in conflict, it's impossible to get to harmony.

The word *harmony* is defined as a pleasant interweaving of parts, an enjoyable combination of differences working together. In music, it is isolated notes that have been beautifully arranged in chords. In other disciplines, a similar notion applies. Literature, for example, is said to be in harmony when separate stories form a single narrative. Paintings and drawings often rely on a harmonious combination of color and line. Legal documents corroborate each other only when their claims will harmonize under scrutiny.

Considering this with marriage in mind, one truth stands out: Difference is a necessity if you want to have harmony. Unless there are two separate entities existing in conflict, it's impossible to get to harmony. This is a key detail many spouses fail to appreciate within marriage.

The beauty of harmony is that delightfulness can come in spite of contradiction. Really, the delight is more potent because of the contradictions. After all, there's nothing significant about two clones getting along.

Dissonant Chords

Students of music know about *dissonance,* when two or more musical notes played simultaneously sound displeasing. They have a clashing effect when they reverberate together; sometimes listeners will cringe or grimace in response to dissonant chords. It's not the sort of tone that would lull you to sleep. Nonetheless, dissonance has a vital place in the arrangement of music. Good composers include the jarring tones in contrast with harmonious ones because when the two are combined, each extreme is more powerful in its own right.

In the presence of harmony, dissonance seems much more grating. Likewise, harmony is considerably more welcome after a spell of dissonance. In fact, even an untrained listener will interpret a dissonant chord as something in need of pleasant resolution. When a pianist or a guitarist plays F-sharp, A-sharp, and B together, audience members will automatically "hear" a solution to that chord—F-sharp and A-sharp in this case—inside their heads. The very nature of dissonance points toward harmony. As notes collide, they suggest that there's something better to be found. In doing so, they lead us to tilt our ears toward the faint, unheard echoes of harmony.

Similarly, all developing marriages will experience moments of dissonance, when the "chords" played by two spouses will be distinctly unpleasant. Remnants of the most recent argument are left to ricochet off the walls. Conflict resounds in the floorboards.

Dissonant interactions like these have the power to disrupt a marriage at its core. If left unresolved, they can split a relationship right down the center. Yet a few of them can be beneficial, and there's an interesting reason why: They hint at the possibility of resolution. Like uncomfortable sound waves bouncing around on an eardrum, they're clues that something better is out there.

Besides wounding individuals and tearing apart a family, there is only one thing that home disharmony does well: It hints there should be something better.

Bumping Elbows

If you've got a glitch in your marital communication or if you're dealing with intense dysfunctions like spousal abuse, it doesn't take rocket science to figure out your marriage isn't harmonious. We probably don't need to tell you that you've got issues to work on. Whether a relationship resounds with dissonance or even if it plays only a few twangy notes here and there, the effects of disharmony are profound. Take heart, though, because in one small way, you're closer to harmony than many other marriages are. Here's why: Although you might not know what you're missing, it's likely you know you're missing *something*.

In many marriages, spouses assume they've found harmony simply because their home isn't filled with rip-roaring brawls like they hear coming from the house next door. Unlike their friends, relatives, and neighbors, these couples don't fight, they don't argue, and they don't raise their voices in conversation. They would never dream of hitting each other—they don't even bump elbows in the hallway. This must be the best kind of harmony, right?

Good Days and Bad

When I (Dan) was growing up, everything in my home revolved around my dad's mood. When he came home after work each night, if he'd had a good day, our evening would be good. When he'd had a good day, we would sit around the dinner table and laugh as a family. He'd tell jokes, and the rest of us would be free to tell jokes too. Our home life could be fun. I especially loved it when my dad had good days because I got to play more basketball on those days. I could be a lighthearted kid out in the yard, shooting hoops without anything to worry about.

On the bad days, it was a different story.

At least a couple times a week, my dad came home upset or angry. Those days, the rest of us would be holding our breath all night, waiting for him to explode and hoping he wouldn't. We knew–my mom, my brother, and me–that any little spark could ignite the rage in him. If that happened, he would start yelling or swinging, at any or all of us. So dinner would be quiet, with one brooding face and three withdrawn ones around the table. There would be no jokes, no fun, only fear and eggshells to walk on.

Wednesdays were especially bad because on Wednesdays we went to church. We'd sit in a pew at our small, legalistic country church and listen to men testify about what was "important" in life— that women should wear only dresses, that women should never cut their hair, etc. I think my dad would get charged up on the strictness and authority of it all because he'd fight with us the whole way home. We never knew how bad it would be—if it would be hollering, demanding, and controlling, or if it would be beating, twisting, squeezing, kicking, bruising, or breaking. I hated Wednesdays.

I can remember as a boy, I would be playing basketball outside most afternoons when I would hear my dad's old Ford truck top the hill that led down to our home. It puttered just loudly enough to make my ears perk up and my heart skip a beat. Would today be a good day or a bad one? Would he be friendly? Would he be happy? Would he have a funny story to tell? Or would there be fear and hurting again?

Not exactly.

Many husbands and wives are living two separate lives under the same roof. They might share a couple of kids and a checking account, but their lives hardly intertwine. She does her thing; he does his. Or one exists at the mercy of the other. They sleep in the same bed at night and eat from the same casserole dish for dinner, but that doesn't mean they have harmony. To take further the music analogy, these people are separate melodies on two totally different compositions. How can they have harmony if they aren't even part of the same song?

> A lack of arguing does not equal harmony.

Minimal controversy does not equal harmony. A lack of arguing does not equal harmony. A wall full of cherub-faced family portraits does not equal harmony. Harmony in the home is a oneness, a togetherness that vibrates throughout the rooms. More than cohabitating, more than sharing the planet, harmony is a mingling of lives. It's that extra little twang that bumps up a marriage from satisfactory to melodic.

How about you and your spouse try making a little music?

Mind Your Marriage Talk

Of all the hurdles on the road to harmony, communication is definitely the biggest. You know what we're talking about—"It's not what you said; it's how you said it." A major part of personal interaction, communication consists of two things: what is said and how we interpret what is said. Most of the time, when people think about improving their communication, they focus on changing their tone of voice and selecting the perfect word and the perfect time to deliver those words. There's no doubt such things are significant. However, there's another vital part of communicating that often is overlooked.

When you speak, you send four kinds of messages to your listeners—and only one of those messages is verbal. While your voice transmits a verbal message, you also convey a large amount of information through your appearance, mannerisms, and physical behavior. These three types of messages are known as nonverbal communication or *body language.*

Research shows that more than half (some research shows up to 70 percent) of communication takes place nonverbally. When you speak one on one or in front of a group, your listeners make an assessment of you and your message based on what they see as well as what they hear. They use their visual impressions to determine if you're sincere, if you *truly* believe what you're saying, if you're interested in them, and if you're confident and comfortable with the situation. In these ways, actions speak much louder than words.

If you want your body to communicate effectively, here are ways you can start:

- Eliminate mannerisms such as pacing, finger tapping, fidgeting, and rocking back and forth. These habits often send messages that are not intentional and can even make listeners feel unimportant, devalued, or flat-out hurt. On top of that, such behaviors tend to distract and annoy people. When your behavior contains mannerisms like these that are unrelated to your spoken message, the actions call attention to themselves and away from your words. On the other hand, when your actions match your words, your words are doubly strong.

- Be genuine, spontaneous, and relational when connecting with your spouse. The single most important rule for making your body language speak effectively is this: Be yourself. Don't try to imitate someone else. Instead, make it your desire to respond naturally in all your communication. People quickly see through false or fake responses, whether they are verbal or behavioral.

- Let your body reflect the way you feel. When you act based on your feelings, you project your real self. If you're interested in your subject and believe in what you're saying, your body language will demonstrate that.

Curbing communication is a great way to minimize disagreements and arguments. At the very least, it helps to settle them faster. When you practice these behaviors in your marital conversations, you take a big step toward home harmony. Still, there's one more necessary element if you want to move in that direction.

Beware the Marriage Balk

Baseball fans know that when a runner is on base the opposing pitcher's stance is very important. With one exception,[13] when the pitcher has started his windup, he is considered "committed to home." This means, in basic terms, he is preparing to pitch a ball in the direction of home plate. If he starts and fails to throw home, instead faking a throw or motioning in any direction other than home plate, this is called a balk, and it's illegal. As a penalty, any and all runners on the field are granted a free pass to the next base. Once the pitcher has committed to home, there are consequences for breaking that commitment. He must follow through.

Marriage, by definition, commits two spouses to home. The act of getting married points their relationship in the direction of forever, and both spouses vow to keep it that way. Still, there are circumstances that can lure one or both of them away from their commitment. Specifically, when conflicts arise, husbands and wives are often tempted to balk. Instead of sticking to it, they break.

Whether they're trying to decide what to have for dinner or figuring out what they'll do when the cancer gets as bad as the doctor predicts it will, they have the option to either focus on home or choose something else. Often it seems much easier to choose something else, so how can a marriage stay committed?

---

13 If the pitcher steps off the rubber with his plant foot and breaks his arms, he is no longer committed to home.

Only Up from Here

We've mentioned golf once already in this book, but in honor of divots everywhere, we thought we'd talk about it again. If you've played the game, you know that beginners can take out a club, swing, and only hope to make contact with the ball. As a novice golfer, you're content if you can manage that single amazing feat. When you move up from the beginner stage to a higher skill level, you try to make contact *and* hit the ball with some semblance of accuracy. (At this phase, you're content with minimal accuracy.)

The next stage is more accuracy—maybe the ball goes where you would like it to go nearly half the time. As you spend more time and effort in playing the game, your ability increases and expectations rise until, as a practiced golfer, you expect to hit the green on a regular basis. Eventually your aim is to consistently hit the ball within a few yards or even a few feet from the hole.

When you first start golfing, you only dream about such accomplishments. Your skills are so poor that you often have a difficult time

Move On

Interestingly enough, a good golf pro will tell you that the final advancement in golf is almost entirely mental. To get your best possible scores, you have to believe you can do it. When you have a bad shot or a bad game, you have to let it go—move on and not try to make up for it on the next shot or in the next game. Keep pressing forward; keep giving yourself a fresh start.

Similarly, your mental game is very important to home harmony. If you mess up the communication in your marriage one day or if you cause a huge conflict with your spouse, you might be tempted to wallow in it. Instead, make things right and then move on. Let the next time be a fresh start, a chance to do better.

enjoying a single nine-hole round. But as you watch the seasoned golfers around you—with their expensive gear, well-worn clubs, and heroic tales from the fairway—you get the sense that these people really *love* the game. They're really good at it, too, and yet you have a slight suspicion that at one time in their lives, they were just as bad at golf as you are.

This closely parallels the life of a marriage. On your wedding day, you march down the aisle together and plan for a really successful go at wedded bliss. You plan to be really good at marriage. Yet about three days after "I do," you discover you're not nearly as skilled as you thought. Symbolically, the golf ball is going all over the place. It's disappointing, frustrating, and painful.

Like golf, marriage is something you have to acquire a knack for. You have to learn the basics and apply them to your relationship. If you don't get the fundamentals under control, you'll never get to where you want to be.

The key to golf and marriage is this: If you can't seem to get where you want to go, don't give up. Keep trying; keep practicing. Stay committed to your goal, to finishing. Know that you're only a beginner, and there's a lot to learn. Don't expect a hole in one on your first swing—that's unrealistic. At first, simply try to make contact with the ball. Then try to get better at making contact, and straighten out your shot a bit. And then try hitting the ball straight sometimes or half of the time.

This doesn't mean you should settle for a bad marriage (or a bad golf game). You shouldn't. But you also shouldn't have expectations that are worlds beyond your ability. Shoot for a realistic target, and keep moving toward it. Keep moving your target too. Getting better is a long process, so enjoy the journey. Enjoy the small improvements along the way.

As you guard home harmony within your marriage, you'll find that you enjoy it more and more. You'll discover a peace you wouldn't have even dreamed of before. You'll get the hang of things, and you'll find that the rewards are worth every single ounce of effort you put into them.

If you don't already, we promise you'll love this someday. It really does get *that* good. It's worth starting, and it's definitely worth playing to the finish. So go ahead, take a swing.

Chapter 8 Follow-up
Guarding Home Harmony

His & Hers:

Multiple choice: Individually, select the response that best fits, then discuss your answers.

He says:

1. When I'm angry or upset, I usually . . .
    a. want to solve the disagreement as soon as possible.
    b. need time by myself so I can cool down.

2. I usually attempt to solve/end disagreements by . . .
    a. yelling.
    b. physical aggression.
    c. discussing them calmly.
    d. ignoring them until they go away.

3. The last time I apologized to my wife was . . .
    a. a few hours ago.
    b. a few days ago.
    c. a few weeks ago.
    d. I can't remember.

4. The last time I should have apologized to my wife was . . .
    a. a few hours ago.
    b. a few days ago.
    c. a few weeks ago.
    d. I can't remember.

5. When there's conflict in our marriage, resolution usually comes because . . .
    a. I initiate it.
    b. my wife initiates it.

    c. we both initiate it at different times.

    d. we don't talk about it; we just hope it will go away.

She says:

1. When I'm angry or upset, I usually . . .
   a. want to solve the disagreement as soon as possible.
   b. need time by myself so I can cool down.

2. I usually attempt to solve/end disagreements by . . .
   a. yelling.
   b. physical aggression.
   c. discussing them calmly.
   d. ignoring them until they go away.

3. The last time I apologized to my husband was . . .
   a. a few hours ago.
   b. a few days ago.
   c. a few weeks ago.
   d. I can't remember.

4. The last time I should have apologized to my husband was . . .
   a. a few hours ago.
   b. a few days ago.
   c. a few weeks ago.
   d. I can't remember.

5. When there's conflict in our marriage, resolution usually comes because . . .
   a. I initiate it.
   b. my husband initiates it.
   c. we both initiate it at different times.
   d. we don't talk about it; we just hope it will go away.

Ask your spouse:

- What's one thing I do that makes our home less harmonious?

- Was there ever a time in our marriage when you felt you weren't very committed to the relationship? Why?

- Do we have unresolved conflict in our marriage?

- Do any of our conflicts keep repeating themselves? If so, what can we do to avoid them in the future?

Guard home harmony this week:

- Before you open the door to your house, make sure you have a good attitude. Give your spouse a big hug and a kiss and say something encouraging to him or her. Watch to see how the tone in your home changes with this simple effort.

THE CONCEPT

Jesus Christ was more than just a nice guy. He was more than a wise Jewish rabbi. He was more than an intelligent teacher. He was more than "was."

You may have had horrible experiences with churches or with church people in the past. You might hate religion, period.

Regardless, Jesus Christ is the hope for your marriage.

Jesus Christ *is* the one thing that can make the most profound impact on all the other areas of you marriage. From the CHDs to the PNDs, from the front porch to the back door, from the bedroom to the blender, and everything in between, He is the answer for whatever you're facing and the hope for keeping it together.

If you really want your marriage to be something, He needs to be your everything.

THE CONSTİTUENTS

Our question isn't to an audience this time—it's to you:

Do you know yet that Jesus Christ can change a marriage, 100 percent?

147

Chapter 9

Building Spiritual Fusion

Prayer was taken out of public schools in 1962. Many people will argue that ever since that decision, life in America has declined significantly. There are statistics everywhere that will show a rise in teenage pregnancy, sexually transmitted diseases, divorce, crime, and physical violence. There's no binding proof that will tie this idea together, but we believe there is some truth to it and we think it's the same something missing in marriages today.

It's not easily definably, but in this final chapter we attempt to explain it. The fact is that without a moral compass to guide them, people in America don't agree on or really know right from wrong. This means everyone develops their own definition which leaves no room for consistency, continuity, or accountability, but plenty of space for chaos and unrest.

The same is true in marriage. If there is no guiding principle or attention on something bigger than ourselves, we often view marriage through the lens of our own needs. We focus our measurement of success on how well our spouse is making us happy. When the depth of perception in the marriage only extends to what someone else is doing, instead of reflecting back on what we are doing, the picture gets distorted. It's not only a short-sighted approach, but there's little opportunity for a bigger picture to emerge. A spouse, living in this reality, rarely sees beyond his or her own needs in order to fuse together with their mate. Even the most compatible of couples will fall short of marital bliss without the infusion of spirituality to serve as a continuous guide that nudges them back on the road to paradise.

The reason we can't achieve this utopia of marriage on our own, is because when it comes to relationships between husbands and wives, there isn't a natural bond strength as resolute as say carbon and oxygen or hydrogen and oxygen. These combinations have elements involved that create a high "bond strength." Once they've become attached, they're difficult to separate; they favor a relationship more than they favor a disconnection.

The opposite is true of people who have a tendency toward separating for the smallest of infractions. That's why they need help in reaching the ultimate goal of staying married for life.

There have been times in my (Dan's) marriage when I was convinced that I had married the wrong person. My relationship with Jane was stuck in a rut, and I didn't see much hope for getting unstuck. Specifically, I didn't see how I could get unstuck with Jane in particular. Some days, it seemed that the two of us were the most mismatched pair on earth.

For starters, she's got the better brain. When we were in college, her grade point average could've muscled mine into oblivion. She worked hard at school and studied day and night for her tests. In comparison, I'd limit my study sessions to the short sidewalk stroll between my dorm room and the classroom on test day.

It's no wonder she got better grades. And she liked to keep it that way. Whenever we had classes together, she wouldn't let me anywhere near her because she didn't want to take the risk that I'd see her answers. She knew I'd cheat like a bandit if I could.

You see, she's honest too! All through our marriage, it's been like this.

Another prime example is that I still haven't caught on to the whole paying-attention thing. My wife, in her charming, Southern-belle way, will politely listen as people drone on with their boring stories. She's even kind enough to ask them questions and prompt *more* droning afterward.

> To develop the first eight steps alone is . . . like going to the ocean and getting only your big toe wet,

I, on the other hand, have a tendency to interrupt when I'm even slightly distracted. Whenever Jane and I go out with other people, she has to put a death grip on my leg so I know when I'm butting in during a conversation. I'm learning to keep my mouth shut, but I'm not nearly as good at it as Jane is. The handprints above my knee will attest to that.

A total mismatch. How in the world can two so very different people actually stay together?

Beyond the Big Toe

There's no doubt the topics we've focused on thus far are significant. Developing the first eight steps in a marriage will improve drastically the relationship between a husband and wife. Your communication skills, sex life, emotional health, personalities, money management, closeness, friendship, and harmony are all important. Still, there's so much more to it! In fact, to develop the first eight steps alone is to limit yourself to a shallow version of wedded bliss. It's like going to the ocean and getting only your big toe wet. If you want to really build an extraordinary marriage, you must wade in further.

In West Michigan, where we're from, a wedding can take place in as little as three days. If two people have a marriage license, a judge, and a couple of witnesses, they can tie the knot in a downtown courthouse on seventy-two hours' notice. They don't need a photographer, a caterer, a planner, a florist, a tailor, a minister, or a chauffeur; as long as a few simple criteria are met, they're good to go. None of the extra trimmings are necessary; just kiss the bride and be on your merry way.

Not surprisingly, very few couples decide to go the no-frills route for their wedding. Even those on a tight budget or a rushed schedule want their wedding to feel ceremonial. We wear special clothing, rent a church, invite family members to witness the event, buy huge scrapbooks to showcase the day's photos, serve a meal afterward, expect presents from guests, and spend obscene amounts of money on a cake. For the most part, we treat the launch of a marriage as if it's a big deal, as if it's beyond ordinary.

And we should. And it is.

Ancient Roots

In ancient Hebrew tradition, marriage was a covenant relationship. More than a legal contract, it was a binding pact between two people, their families, and God Himself. Marriage wasn't about romantic love expressed between two spouses; rather, it was a commitment that stemmed out of love and devotion to God. A man and a woman joined their lives with the understanding that marriage made them one in God's eyes. This was no small step because they knew a marriage of *one* was very different from a marriage of *two*.[14]

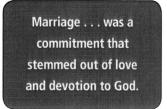

Marriage . . . was a commitment that stemmed out of love and devotion to God.

For the ancient Hebrews, becoming one had ramifications that worked in two directions. First, there were benefits: If a husband and wife saw themselves as a single unit, each of them would work toward the good of the unit rather than toward their own individual good. The husband would learn to love his wife because she had become a part of himself. The wife would love her husband because he had

---

14 For more information on traditions like these, good sources include James Garlow's *The Covenant* (Kansas City: Beacon Hill Press, 1999), and resources by That the World May Know Ministries (www.followtheirabbi.com).

become a part of herself. Imagine the strength and security found in such an arrangement—anything that harmed one harmed the other, and anything that benefited one benefited the other. Acting selfishly became senseless because it denied half of the new self. This went far beyond a simple "I do" and a new last name for the wife. Entire identities changed, each one made stronger by the adoption of the other.

Parallel to these benefits, however, were severe consequences for breaking marriage vows. As we've already mentioned, when a Hebrew bride and groom were wed, they understood their relationship as an outgrowth of their commitment to God. Thus, without each other, the two—the *one*—would no longer be considered whole in His eyes. Unfaithfulness to a spouse was also unfaithfulness to God. Ending a marriage would represent disobedience, even defiance of God Himself. For such actions, penalties were great. It was the kind of thing that made people take a relationship seriously.

Compared to the ancient Hebrews, we treat marriage quite differently these days. Although we're very good at inserting religious elements into our weddings—a prayer here, a hymn there, the Bible's Love Chapter embossed on the programs—we haven't proved very successful at incorporating God, through a relationship with Jesus Christ, into our marriages. In fact, for many couples, the wedding ceremony encompasses the only spiritual notes their marriage will ever play. Many couples prefer it that way.

There are husbands and wives who prefer to keep their marriage void of any sign of religion or spirituality. Although the man or woman might hold individual beliefs or practices, they are reluctant to come together in those. Instead, they maintain disconnection, like his-and-hers towels. As long as both people can get along, who cares if they have differences, right? Why throw all the complications of religion into an already good thing?

Sadly, of all the things couples like these have figured out in their marriage, they've missed the most necessary part. They might have a good thing going, but they're nowhere near the road to greatness. Why? Because they've denied themselves spiritual fusion. It's like climbing a mountain and stopping short of the peak. You cheat yourself out of the spectacular view that you could have had with a little more effort. You settled for less. The view was nice, but not the best. That's what will happen in your marriage if you stop short of this final step.

A Roadster with Wheels

If you haven't tuned into the spiritual element of your marriage, the focus of this chapter might seem far-fetched. You might find it hard to believe that spiritual beliefs can make a real difference in your relationship with your spouse. That's understandable. In fact, both of us felt the exact same way at certain points in our own relationships.

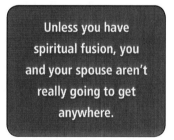

Unless you have spiritual fusion, you and your spouse aren't really going to get anywhere.

In spite of our respective fears and discomforts, though, we've both worked at building spiritual fusion with our wives. In the process, we've both individually concluded that fusion is the one ingredient truly necessary for husbands and wives. Sure, marriage is an arrangement in which people communicate, have sex, pay bills, and try to figure out how to be a team. And personalities, emotions, and gender play roles in marriage. All of those are important to talk about. But building a marriage on those elements alone is like building a Lamborghini without giving it wheels. The car will look nice and run great, but where's it going?

In the same way, you can have a marriage with home harmony, cherishing attitudes, sexual satisfaction, and the like, but unless you have spiritual fusion, you and your spouse aren't really going to get anywhere. If you skip the effort and stick to things like the first eight steps, you might be happy. You'll probably have a lovely marriage, and it will be without all the fuss of two becoming one. Who wouldn't want that?

Our goal in writing this book has been to help you get your marriage's engine purring, to help you get its plugs sparking, and to help you make sure you've got oil to spare in your relationship. But we also want to help give you a set of wheels, so you and your spouse can really get somewhere together. Fusion is where the wheels come in.

A Change in Focus

Early in their marriage, Melissa and Steve were given some advice from a friend about praying together as a couple. This friend had told them it would deepen and strengthen their relationship. "There's so much more!" he'd said. At first, they were skeptical and uncomfortable with the idea. Although both were Christians and had grown up with Christian parents, neither Melissa nor Steve had been taught to pray specifically as spouses. *How will that work?* they wondered.

Their friend kept pushing them to try it, though, promising that praying together as a couple would revolutionize their marriage. After a few months of his prodding, they decided to try. They wanted to make their marriage better, to feel closer and more connected. Still, getting started proved more complicated than they had thought. Questions dominated in the beginning: What should they do? What could they pray about? How long did they have to pray? Should they talk first? If so, who should jump-start the conversation? Did the husband have to lead, or should the wife? Should they take turns? What was the formula?

Despite their questions, the couple began praying together some nights before they went to sleep. To their surprise, it was easier than they had thought it would be. Their list of things to pray about opened up, and they discovered a wealth of topics and concerns they wanted to talk with God about—family, church, work, each other, friends, and big decisions. Gradually, praying together became a pattern in their marriage, although they'll admit they hit potholes in the beginning. These days, a running joke between the two of them is that twice Melissa fell asleep while Steve was praying for her. "I could hardly believe it," he says. "Why was I praying if she wasn't listening?" She sees things differently. "It was just so peaceful to hear him pray!" she says with a laugh. "I can't believe he didn't take it as a compliment."

Still, regardless of difficulties and the occasional snooze, Melissa and Steve kept making prayer a priority in their marriage. Several years and four children later, they can't imagine where they'd be without it. What began somewhat awkwardly became a routine, then a staple, then a foundation. Praying together has changed everything, Melissa and Steve report—from the way they argue and the way they parent to the way they view each other and the way they forgive.

Why have things in their marriage changed so drastically? It's simple. "When our focus is on Jesus Christ and things that are so pure and right," Melissa explains, "that makes us think differently about earthly things—they're so small. It humbles us; we catch ourselves when we're being trivial." Steve agrees. "We can see each other's view now," he says. "We're not trying to win so much."

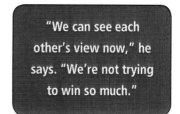

"We can see each other's view now," he says. "We're not trying to win so much."

To observe this couple in their relationship is to see a marriage progressing the way it should. It's like watching two people move from ordinary to extraordinary. Because Melissa and Steve are building spiritual fusion, they're learning to value putting each other first. Above all else, this is what gives them the desire to become more *one* than *two*. As a result, they're even learning how to share hobbies. "She's picking up golf," he says. "I'm trying to get better at shopping."

The Catch-22

The brilliance of spiritual fusion lies in its mystery. There's something unknowable about it, something that can't be captured or explained on paper. Those who've glimpsed fusion—people like Melissa and Steve— know that it radiates all around, a dominating presence that weaves through the health of a marriage. Yet to those who haven't been through fusion, this mystery is merely a faint shadow on a distant wall. Such couples can't understand it, they can barely see it, and they're certainly not living under its influence. Their reality doesn't make a space for fusion, and how could it? How can they clear a way for something they're not even aware of?

This is a saddening catch-22 for many couples: Although unending layers of a marriage's vitality remain unexplored, the two spouses are oblivious to exploration in the first place. Instead, they stick to the well-worn path. They work to develop noble qualities such as financial security, home harmony, and sexual satisfaction. They become happy and content, yet they never take their marriage into that next dimension. They miss out. It's the difference between eating a banana straight off the tree in Ecuador and eating one that was force-ripened on a refrigerated truck along the interstate.

It's hard for couples like these to understand how fusion changes everything. They don't comprehend the countless ways fusion will unlock their world. They can't even begin to fathom that it would prop open the door to a whole new depth of being. They're limited by their limited vision. Until they learn to zoom out and zoom in, ignorance is bliss.

Working toward Fusion

If you as a couple are missing out on spiritual fusion, here are suggestions to help you move toward that goal:

- Make God a part of your conversations. Ask each other questions:
  1. What would you be afraid to ask God?
  2. What do you believe about _____?
  3. Is there anything you see in me that God would want to help me change?
- Read portions of the Bible together, stopping to talk about what you've read and what it tells you about God.

- Hold hands and pray together about a troublesome area of your relationship.
- Go for a walk together and talk about God's creation.
- Attend a place of worship that leaves you both spiritually "fed."

Atypical Means

Too often in marriages, couples try to improve their relationship or numb its pain by using typical means. *Change my marriage,* they say to a counselor. *Change my circumstances,* they say to a pastor. *Change*

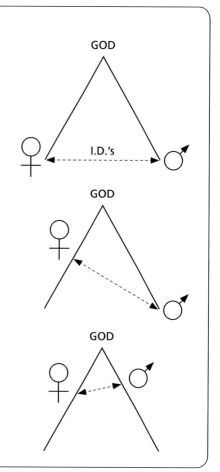

Toward God

When spouses ignore God and try to work out their relationship on their own (horizontally), they quickly find there's a big space between the two of them. In divorce court, that space is called irreconcilable differences.

When one person in the relationship seeks to grow toward God but the other doesn't, the space between the two spouses barely decreases.

But when both spouses grow toward God, they also move closer to each other. The space that divides them shrinks quickly. This is the beauty of spiritual fusion.

my dissatisfaction, they say to a lover, a drug, a bottle, or a distraction. *Change yourself,* they say to their spouse. All these can lead to change in a marriage, but none of them leads to total solution. It's only when they pursue God, through a relationship with Jesus Christ, can they understand why.

In the presence of the One who is fully true, noble, right, pure, lovely, and admirable, our perspective shifts. It simply happens; nobody can avoid it. All our shallowness, selfishness, trite arguments, and faults come to light when we get to know Jesus Christ. Everything else filters through, bubbles to the surface, and pops. Then and only then can we see the solution in marriage: *Change me.*

Change me in my relationship. *Change me* in my actions toward my spouse. *Change me* in the ways I define and seek happiness. *Change me* and my one-sided desires for satisfaction and gratification. *Change me* and my self-centered reasons for sticking it out. *Change me.*

Fusion requires only two things: first, our inability to make a marriage work, and second, our reliance on Jesus Christ to make a marriage work—to make it a success.

Two Requirements

Imagine a marriage in which both the husband and wife are willing to mold themselves for the good of the relationship. Such a marriage is possible with—you guessed it—spiritual fusion. But how do you get there?

You don't access spiritual fusion by pursuing it. A treasure map mentality won't get you there. In fact, fusion is a result of seeking something far greater: inviting Jesus Christ to be a part of your marriage. The Man Upstairs is the real prize, you could say; fusion is icing on the cake. Having a relationship with Jesus Christ is what inspires true change in us, and that, in turn, is what makes fusion possible.

A couple can stay together and enjoy their connection, not because both people are extremely compatible and agreeable but because there is a catalyst tough enough to fuse them together in spite of themselves. When a husband and wife make Jesus Christ the center of their marriage, they begin to take on qualities that earlier had been out of reach. They find that in light of God's grace they have less of a desire to settle scores in their marriage. After experiencing the love of Christ, it's easier for them to extend real love to each other. Having witnessed God's faithfulness, *"til death do us part"* can seem more realistic. Having encountered the forgiveness of Christ, they will be more likely to forgive each other.

Knowing God is what inspires true change in us, and that in turn, is what makes fusion possible.

Perhaps you expected a recipe in this chapter or something like five foolproof steps to fusion. We don't have anything like that. For each marriage, fusion could look drastically different except for one part—a relationship with Jesus Christ and a commitment to keep Him the central part of your relationship.

Fusion is still beyond our comprehension, and this chapter merely scratches the surface, but we know enough to know it's significant and worth passing on. Even though we can't fully capture it on paper, it captivates in real life.

As a final note, we're not gonna lie to you; it's possible to have a nice marriage without all this. You and your spouse can feel as happy as clams without God in your marriage. But once you get a taste of spiritual fusion, you'll never want to go back to the way things were before. Try it out; you'll see. Without Jesus Christ in your marriage, the best you'll ever have is a nice love story, but with Him, you're on your way to a great romance.

Chapter 9 Follow-up
Building Spiritual Fusion

His & Hers:

Respond individually, then discuss your responses:

He says:

On the diagram, mark the places where you think you and your wife currently are when it comes to spiritual fusion.

On the diagram, mark the places where you would like you and your wife to be when it comes to spiritual fusion.

She says:

On the diagram, mark the places where you think you and your husband currently are when it comes to spiritual fusion.

On the diagram, mark the places where you would like you and your husband to be when it comes to spiritual fusion.

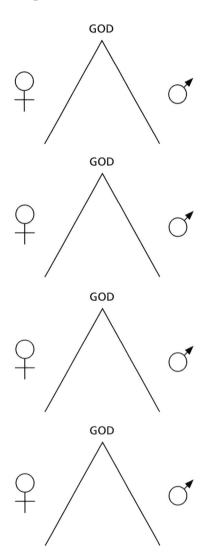

Ask your spouse:

- In what ways could spiritual fusion bring us closer?

- In what ways could we incorporate spiritual fusion into our marriage?

- Before we can build spiritual fusion together, we need to each have a solid relationship with Jesus Christ? Do you believe you have that?

Build spiritual fusion this week:

- Select one area of your marriage that could benefit from spiritual fusion, and discuss the roadblocks you often encounter in that area. Then, as a couple, pray for each other, that God will give you the strength to work past those roadblocks.

Epilogue
A Note from the Authors

We believe that Jesus Christ makes the difference in a home. We've experienced it ourselves. Our marriages aren't perfect by any means, but because we're seeking to follow Christ, we know they are far better than what they could be.

Our relationship with Christ began as it can begin for you:

- By recognizing that God created you and has a purpose for your life.
- By admitting that, on your own, you've failed at that purpose, and you need Christ's forgiveness and guidance to get on track.

In acknowledging these things to God, you become His child and join us on His exciting journey. There is no greater adventure in life than this.

If you make a new decision to follow Christ, please let us know so we can send you materials to support you in your decision. Visit www.WinningAtHome.com to contact us with your questions or stories.